Christian Focus in a Blurry World

Christian Focus in a Blurry World

RAMI DONAHOE, M.S.

Published by Best Seller Publishing®, St. Augustine, FL
Best Seller Publishing® is a registered trademark.
Printed in the United States of America.
ISBN: 978-1-956649-68-0

For more information, please write:
Best Seller Publishing®
53 Marine Street
St. Augustine, FL 32084
or call 1 (626) 765-9750
Visit us online at: www.BestSellerPublishing.org

CONTENTS

INTRODUCTION

Succeeding in life feels like a completely lost art these days. From the overwhelming stress and worry that comes from your work life to trying to figure out if what you're doing is in alignment with your passions and purpose, it can all be a bit too much for so many. Talking about what sets your soul on fire can feel like you're just rubbing your soul raw searching for the answer. Many people in their twenties and older feel compelled to do a lot of things just to ensure they can report back to relatives or friends with similar influential status, and too often, lack that feeling of completing something for their own self-worth.

Succeeding is an art that you create in your life by focusing on what you love instead of focusing on how many things you can do in a day. Remember the elementary school saying: "it's not quantity of work, it's quality of work," that's what we are getting at here. We can get too wrapped up in feeling like we've accomplished a lot of things, but did your day produce anything that moved you closer to achieving your big dream or passion? While it is important to get things accomplished, it is also important to have long term goals for your future, as where and what you are doing today will create what you have and who you are next month, next year and five years from now. Adding more confusion, and possibly more clarity, was Covid-19. Some people used this pandemic time to be flexible and create options for their careers and enhanced their life expectations, such as discovering what their passions in life really were, investing in more time with family, and leaving the job that did not align with their awakening values, dreams and goals. Technology became integral to communication for educational institutions and enabled people to feel a sense of safety at home. While there were a lot of challenges during Covid-19, there were also people who saw the opportunity for growth, such as that mom who finally finished her Bachelor's Degree online or the family that realized their kids may benefit from a more individualized learning program through homeschooling.

This pandemic delivered a lot of challenges and losses such as losing loved ones, becoming seriously ill, being forced to take a stand for your health care decisions and possibly losing your job. Making it through social distancing, masking, caring for loved ones, and just staying alive are all success stories. You're still alive and we celebrate this success!

Coming out of the brain fog that was Covid-19 and realizing your goals and passions are still waiting for you, and that you are a survivor, is highly motivating. Your goals, dreams and calling in Christ Jesus are still waiting for you to make them become reality. As a former School Counselor, I can give you all the positive mindset tools, affirmations and meditations you could need. But it will never be a substitute for the supernatural power of Abba Father, Jesus Christ, and the Holy Spirit. Simply by connecting and allowing God the freedom to move in your life is operating on the highest level of your soul, mind and body. This book is designed to help you gain your focus back and get out of the blur that was Covid-19 with a Biblical perspective. Give yourself permission to plan, create and clear any doubt surrounding your future success. Trusting in God is the most important mindset that a person can have, because we can't control events that happen, however we can choose to have a Proverbs 3:5,6 mindset: "Trust in the Lord with all your heart and lean not on your own understanding; in all your ways submit to Him, and

He will make your paths straight." We can also choose to make wise decisions by "walking with the wise people, as a companion of fools suffers harm."(Proverbs 13:20) Now is your time to carpe-diem-this. Thank you for resetting your life with God and acknowledging He is the source. You will win if you are focused on Him.

Do you struggle with figuring out if you're in alignment with God? Are you searching for answers about what to do with your life and coming up with nothing?

Do you feel like things are in the way and preventing you from your calling? Are you a God-fearing woman or man who is just trying to live in a way that honors Him?

Most importantly, do you feel like you have more gifts to give the world and have absolutely no idea where to be to tap into them? When tapped into and living fully in your everyday life, your Heavenly blessings will open up so much passion and purpose in every aspect of your life.

Yet so many people have no idea where to begin to start accessing the deep and profound spiritual power that comes with that kind of on-purpose living focused on Jesus Christ. You may find yourself struggling to make ends meet and feeling like there's nothing left within you to give those you love—and most importantly, give yourself at the end of the day.

At Positive Space, we want you to succeed in every aspect of your life. We get excited when you succeed. After years of helping people discover their truth, realize their gifts, and own their passion and purpose, we understand that the best way to predict your future is to keep moving and create it with God. Our mission is to help you surrender your past pains to God, align with God in your present, and surface profound clarity to cultivate a wonderful, Spirit led future.

We know that there will be bumps and challenging times in life, especially the more you step out of your stress, worry, trapped feelings and mindset that have held you back. The bigger game you're playing in life, the higher the stakes, also means that when you're at your highest is when the devil will try to knock you down. Those bumps and setbacks are simply just that—bumps and setbacks. You need to see the bigger picture more than simply the "problem" that is happening, but you have a "promise" from the Lord that you can do all things through Christ who strengthens you! (Philippians 4:13)

This book not only helps you focus on your passions, it also identifies things that prevent you from aligning with your goals. Many things may try to stand in your way by hindering your creativity and freedom. Relationships that are unhealthy, unproductive beliefs, and harmful patterns result in getting farther away from what God has for you. When you are far from the Lord it becomes almost impossible to feel comfortable in your own skin because you will produce feelings of guilt, sadness and loneliness. These negative feelings will stand in the way of reaching out to God and renewing yourself in Him, because why would He want to talk to you while you are messing up, making wrong choices and intentionally ignoring Him? This is what the Devil, the liar, will tell you. Don't believe his lies. God always wants you to talk to Him and He will always take you where you are at, as He sent His only Son for you. (John 3:16) Get rid of these negative feelings by talking to the Lord and by bringing your focus back on Him rather than short term temporary experiences. It's time that you have the tools and understanding to tap into your inner strength and become resilient in the face of life's punches by focusing on Jesus Christ. You can create and live the life you've always wanted. It's time you are able to become the unstoppable force of light, love, and empowerment that you were born to be. It's time that you unlock your full potential and give yourself permission to live it every day for the rest of your life.

This book, *Christian Focus In A Blurry World*, is designed to become the ultimate toolkit for tapping into your full potential, stopping the negativity, stress, and anxiety that's holding you back, and stepping into your purpose and passion with power and commitment.

You can do this knowing that God is fighting for you every step of the way, that He's protecting and guiding you, and that there is nothing you can't do with Him providing you with strength and guidance. Even when you can't see the plan in front of you, it's there: "We walk by faith, not by sight." (2 Corinthians 5:7)

Having a positive mindset is crucial to your resilience and success, but that alone will not give you the complete set of tools to live life to your full potential. The truth of your journey is that God (Abba Father), Jesus Christ (The Son Of The Living God), and the Holy Spirit (Living In You) are the supernatural powers that will enable you to surrender fears, anxiety, and painful past hurts that have until now stopped you in areas of your life. The very things that have prevented you from living your greatest version of yourself, from living your best life, are easily eradicated and overcome through the power of God. We call this the Proverbs 3:5 mindset as the focus is all about trusting in the Lord's purpose for you and leaning in to what God has for you, instead of going by what we see in the physical world or what we understand it to be. As long as we are acknowledging Him, He will make our path straight.

This book will become the ultimate roadmap to stepping out of the pains of your past and into the truth deep within you so that you can live the life you've always wanted and get out of your own way, your own understanding.

Are you ready to dive in and discover the raw truth of who you are, why you do what you do, and the many God-given gifts that lie undiscovered within you, waiting to be unleashed on the world? Are you ready to identify thoughts, relationships and beliefs that are preventing you from conquering these brilliant goals? Then, let's dive into *Christian Focus In A Blurry World* and take the first step to unlocking your full potential, overcoming your fears, pains of the past, and anxieties so you can have life finally conspire on your behalf with God leading the way. Your dreams are worth it. God knows the desires of your heart and He longs for you to come closer to Him. The Lord commands that you delight in Him, give gratitude to Him, and this will lead your way to peace and alignment in Christ (Psalm 37:4)

After each chapter in *Christian Focus In A Blurry World*, you're going to be prompted to spend some time with the practices, thoughts, and realizations that come up as you go on this journey to creating a life you love. Take five to ten minutes on each prompt to journal and use some relaxing music that allows you to process your thoughts. Let's dive right in to your life now that it is finally coming into focus.

CHAPTER ONE

SOME REFLECTIONS TO GUIDE YOU

Take time to invest in a journal to ensure you will be able to work through this first chapter and gain the best results from this process. You will want to write down your thoughts and keep a record of what is really permeating your mind. Understanding where to begin to change your life can feel like you're stuck in a blizzard trying to find a polar bear. You're looking in every direction, only to be more lost than you were a moment ago. Every time you take a step forward, you don't know if you're actually going forward or taking two steps backward. With all the cognitive interference, also known as constant interruptions, please take time to give yourself permission to read through this book and identify where you are, what you desire, and what God is saying to you.

To get out of the overwhelming and painful blizzard, you first have to be able to honestly and openly take some time for reflection on your life as it currently is. Looking at who you are, why you do what you do, and the things that you find the most joy and happiness in, as well as the most pain and trauma, can be not only eye-opening, but also freeing.

This chapter is designed to help you better understand where you're at in your life, the way in which you view the world, and help provide you with some spiritual clarity that will open your mind, body, and soul up to all the unique gifts that God has in His plan for your life. They're already there waiting for you. Isn't it time you stepped into everything these gifts have to offer to your life?

Here are some of our favorite guiding questions to gain a better understanding and self-awareness in your life so you can start down the road to unlocking your full potential.

What were your biggest successes in life?

This is an important topic to consider no matter what stage you're at in your life. When something great happens, do you take time to appreciate it for what it is, or do you lose yourself in the moments of success? Letting things get to your head can derail you. So can over-thinking everything that happens even when it's good. Celebrate the wonderful things about you.

Take some time to reflect and focus on what you feel are the biggest successes in your life so far. What is it about them that makes them a success for you? What are the feelings that come up around those times for you? Why do you consider them your biggest successes? Can you devote 5-10 minutes every day to express your gratitude to God? Write down your thoughts in your journal as they come to you, giving yourself permission to feel joy about these successes.

What brought you the most happiness?

If you take a long hard look, where were you most successful in your life? You'll discover that your happiest moments tend to be found there, too. There's a reason for this. If you're truly living in tune with what you are called to do in this life and using your gifts to inspire others, you're tapping into authentic joy and creating your very own Positive Space. God wants you to think on good and happy things. "Finally, brothers and sisters, whatever is true, whatever is noble, whatever is right, whatever is pure, whatever is lovely, whatever is admirable if anything is excellent or praiseworthy think about such things." (Philippians 4:8)

Find the moments in your life that brought you the most happiness and look at what you were doing. What about those moments made you so happy? What were you doing? Were you giving back to others, creating a piece of art, telling a story, or building your business? Whatever it is, these moments and memories of happiness and success are, in most cases, directly tied to the spiritual gifts that are given to you by God.

Discovering what you were created for by the Creator is one of the most freeing experiences in your life. Searching these moments can help shed some light as you reflect on your life so far. Having an understanding of your purpose though Christ Jesus will allow you to stay on track in this relay of life rather than taking needless detours that you were not called to take in the first place. Take time to journal about your memories of what moments made you the most happy.

What were the best choices you have made?

Can you see where we're going with these questions? So many people often spend most of their time during the day focusing on their failures, letting fear take control, and listening to the negative self-talk that stops them from living their best lives and achieving their full potential. By taking the time to stop and reflect on your life up till now and focusing on the positive experiences, you can transform your mindset to see those moments for everything remarkable that they are.

It's often said when you're growing up that it takes ten positively charged emotional experiences to erase just one negatively charged emotional experience. And when you stop and reflect on this exercise, you can see that firsthand.

Take a few minutes and look at the best choices you made. Then, really focus on the feelings that were around those choices, and especially as to why you made them. What was it about the reason you made those choices that stands out? How did those choices impact the rest of your life in that time period? Take time to write and reflect your thoughts and feelings in your journal.

What were your favorite experiences?

This is a fun one. It's essential to spend time reflecting on the successes and choices that have led you to happiness and look at your most memorable, favorite experiences. What was it about those experiences that made them so much fun?

What were you doing? Really look at the feelings that remembering those experiences bring up for you. The gifts you were born with and are meant to be shared with the rest of us in the world are found in these kinds of experiences. When you're living in complete alignment with your gifts, His plan, and your passion and purpose, you'll end up having the best time of your life, no matter what you're doing. But, many people don't realize that's exactly what's happening when they have their favorite experiences. Take time to really observe any patterns of happiness, joy and fulfillment and continue to write these thoughts and events in your journal.

Did you have a spiritual encounter?

That same feeling we talked about above can lead to a spiritual encounter. Have you ever had one of these in your life? Reflect in your journal on what that was like for you and what you were doing when it happened.

What did you learn about the world?

As you've been reflecting on your successes, joy, and experiences, what are some things that you have learned about the world in that time? What have you learned about how you fit into the world around you?

What have you learned about yourself?

Everything you've been reflecting on so far plays a part in who you are. Your choices and experiences influence the person you've become. Likewise, what you experience has an impact on the way in which you see and interpret the world around you. So, throughout the course of your life and with everything that has brought you pain, joy, and happiness, what is it that you have learned about yourself, what you really desire, and who you really are in your own skin?

What were your best memories?

These can be anything from experiences to childhood memories of moments with your friends, family, and parents. Write down some of the best memories that you can recall? When you're really tuned in, as they say, you will find that you have an innate ability to recall memories from your childhood that you haven't remembered in years.

What people did you enjoy connecting with?

There are people you have a deep and profound connection with throughout your life. Who are those people, and what is it about that connection with them that stands out to you? Please take time to reflect on the loving, positive people in your life and write down their names in your journal. Say a prayer for each one of them in thanks and gratitude to God.

NEXT... WHAT ARE YOU FEEDING YOUR ENERGY TO?

Have you ever heard the expression that you are who you surround yourself with? Or maybe you've heard the one about how the energy you put out into the world comes back to you eventually. However it's worded, both of those are saying that you can choose what you feed your energy and what you put your energy into.

You can choose to focus on your pain, fears, and self-doubt and continue to feed those. But unfortunately, doing so can lead you down a path where you're constantly surrounded by negativity, pain, and feeling trapped in a life you don't want to live. It is stated in the Bible: "Therefore do not worry about tomorrow, for tomorrow will worry about itself. Each day has enough trouble of its own." (Matthew 6:34) God is telling you to focus on today and let Him handle tomorrow. To truly tap into your full potential in life, you need to be conscious of the worries, people, and even careers that you're feeding your energy to. If you're always investing time in toxic people, worrying, and useless patterns, guess what is going to come back to you and constantly resurface in your life? Proverbs 13:20 further validates our emphasis on what and who you surround yourself with: "Walk with the wise and become wise, for a companion of fools suffers harm."

If all your energy is being sucked by your current job that you don't even enjoy, you've got nothing left to focus on the things that you actually love doing. What you invest your energy into matters. It's essential because what you are investing and creating now is who you will be in a few years, next year and tomorrow.

It's true what they say about when you love what you're doing, you'll never work a day in your life again. So, take some time to look at the people, things, experiences, and work that you're investing your time and energy into.

Does it fulfill you?

Does it or the people contribute to you and your happiness?

Are you happy?

Are you living a life you love?

If not, then where can you focus your energy so that you are?

Take time to answer these questions in your journal.

YOU WERE CREATED BY GOD, WHO IS THE MASTER CREATOR...

We were all created for a purpose. Something bigger than who we are as individuals. There are gifts within us all that are meant to be shared with the world. They are why He created us and put us in this world and in this time.

After all, He Created the Heavens and Earth, and man, as it says in Genesis 1:27, "So God created man in His own image, in the image of God He created him." Man or woman, there is a reason for His creation, and when you're living your truth with purpose and passion and at your highest potential possible, you are tapped into those God-given gifts. There's no greater joy than that which comes from sharing your gifts from God with the world.

If you were created for sharing the gifts and purpose within you with the world, what's holding you back from stepping into the glory that lies ahead for you? The truth is, there are many things, and that's exactly what this book is going to dive into throughout each chapter.

YOU WERE GIVEN LIFE FOR A GLORIOUS REASON!

In Jeremiah 29:11, the Lord declares, "For I know the plans I have for you. Plans to prosper you and not to harm you, plans to give you hope and a future."

If all of that glory is yours for the taking, if you've been blessed with that kind of Heaven-sent glory, then it's time you finally take hold of that, surrender to His plan, and step powerfully into your passion and purpose.

But it's not quite that easy after all, is it? For many, it can take their entire lives to truly step into the person they were born to be and to tap into their God-given gifts and abilities. But designing your life in alignment with your passions and God's purpose for your life isn't some secret locked deep within the depths of a cave to which there's no map to find. Instead, it's right in front of you, and it's yours for the taking.

Are you ready?

Take a look at all you have accomplished in life or even over the past year.

It's always better to start small and open your vision wider as you go. Stop and really search inside yourself to look at all the things that you have accomplished over the past year. And by accomplishments, I don't mean just focusing on the most significant things. Accomplishments that you're proud of can be as simple as getting through a week managing three kids, their after-school activities, a full-time job, and still being able to provide everyone with everything they need, and even have time for yourself.

So many people that I work with struggle with recognizing their accomplishments. They can't see beyond their fears, self-doubts, and stressors to really understand just how significant the small accomplishments actually are in their lives. If you aren't taking the time to celebrate the small victories and soak in the gratitude that you feel for those moments in your life, how can you possibly appreciate and even realize the larger successes and accomplishments that come into your life?

The truth is that you can't. So often, our vision is blurred by the pains of our past, the traumas, and judgements from our childhood that don't acknowledge and celebrate all the things the Lord enabled you to accomplish thus far. You might have missed just how amazing of a person you are.

Take some time and examine the smallest accomplishments from the past year. Look at what they opened up for you in your life. Did you communicate with God? Even on the simplest level: "God help me please." Did you ever spot the Lord helping you as you were accomplishing small to large goals? Was there a family routine, career event, adventure or spiritual occurrence that can help you identify what you are most passionate about in life, so much so that you feel the very construct of time seems to disappear?

Take time to journal and reflect on something you have done when time got away from you because you enjoyed it so much.

Now, take time to look at what you would like to change.

So if you've written down some of your accomplishments from the past year or even longer, now it's time to look at the things you would like to change in your life. The negatively charged emotions and realities of your life.

What are they? What do you want to change in your life? What are the things that you would like more of? And, no, we don't mean money and power. What emotions, feelings, and inspirations would you like more often in your life? What type of relationships would you like to invest more time into and continue developing and growing? Where have you grown spiritually? What service have you given to your community? Take time to reflect in your journal.

It's essential to live a fruitful and passionate life to invest your time into the things you love. When you're putting the majority of time into the things you love and allowing yourself to share your gifts with the world, you're literally designing your life. You've designed your routine, the tribe you spend time with, your relationships, and the activities that you spend time doing in such a way that you're really alive and living in harmony with God. You're living in tune with God's plan for your life, and the world around you is conspiring on your behalf. A negative God-does-not-exist-so-I-gotta-make-it-happen mindset will keep you in bondage to everyone else's control. A negative attitude like this is both asserting too much power over one's self and also denying that the Creator is able to supernaturally intervene and intercede in your life. A positive Proverbs 3:5 trust-in-God mindset will take the unneeded stress off of you and will communicate to God that His grace is sufficient: "Trust in the Lord with all your heart and lean not on your own understanding; in all your ways submit to Him, and He will make your paths straight."

We can try to control everything in our environment, but realistically, we will fall short every time and end up feeling unsatisfied without asking for the help of God. One of my most used quotes is: "I'm at my best when I am at my worst." This is possible because when I am at my worst, I have no more options that my mind has created and my human possibilities come to an end. At that dismal point I would start to pray to God for intervention, and He always intervenes and pulls me out of the pit of despair. Paul says, "But He said to me, 'My grace is sufficient for you, for my power is made perfect in weakness.' Therefore, I will boast all the more gladly about my weaknesses, so that Christ's power may rest on me. That is why, for Christ's sake, I delight in weaknesses, in insults, in hardships, in persecutions, in difficulties. For when I am weak, then I am strong."

And that line of thinking takes us right into the next part of designing your life...

CHAPTER TWO

THE THEME AND PURPOSE FOR YOUR LIFE

Having a theme for your life is incredibly impactful in your daily life, your relationships, and who you are at your core.

That's exactly why I feel it's critical to include it here in *Christian Focus In A Blurry World*. Think about it this way… Every movie or even episode on TV that you watch contains a theme. Movies especially. The theme of every movie is something as simple as "Life is like a box of chocolates. You never know what you're going to get." That iconic line resonates on so many levels, and as you watch a film with that theme, you see the characters explore the idea that you never know what life has in store for you, but the more you live it fully, the more life you're able to experience. Trying to understand what life has in store and what your future holds is a never-ending battle you have no chance whatsoever of winning.

So as in a movie, the theme of your life matters. So, for example, you could want your theme to be Alive, Creative, and Humble. And so, you live a life in such a way that you constantly find yourself feeling alive, creative, and humble. But it doesn't just stop with you. It's about sharing that energy and being that space in your life for everyone else around you.

Creating a theme for your life helps you have a crystal-clear vision around the things you want and the things that don't serve or help you. The more you can shed away the things that aren't healthy for you, such as relationships, social media, certain television and movie selections and negative self-talk, the easier it becomes to design your life.

Think about the Lord and His will for you, the passion and gifts you are seeing and experiencing in your life. What is your theme for your life? At this point, please take time to pray and ask for guidance from the Holy Spirit.

Take time to journal **at least** two strengths that you have such as: integrity, honesty, creativity, enthusiastic presence, passion, patience, loyalty, teamwork mindset, communication, dependability, eagerness to learn, courage, intuition, empathy, art, persuasive ability and listening skills. These are just examples to aid you in finding words to develop your personal theme for your beautiful life.

Next, take time to write two ways you truly feel joy expressing these strengths with others, for example: supporting, producing, creating, writing, acting, cooking, feeding, learning, teaching, editing, filming, leading, speaking, singing, traveling, researching, developing, nurturing, helping, designing, influencing, shaping, building, drawing and constructing.

Lastly, combine these two strengths with how you achieve joy and create your theme for life, for your Positive Space. For example: "My theme is to create media and products to inspire people to have a relationship or get closer to God," "My theme is to use my artistic abilities to communicate the power of love and acceptance to all people and living creatures" and "My theme is to write books that influence people to give up drug addictions and find peace through Jesus Christ."

Take time to turn on some calming worship music and spend time in the quiet place of the Most High God while you bring your theme statement to life.

What do you want the theme of your life to be? Write it down and live it! Even if it is just three words, you still have a great beginning and a tool to use to keep you on the right path.

The social media blur that wants to take away your purpose.

Posting on social media is addictive and impulse driven. Before you post, take your theme and pair it with what you are about to post. If your theme is a simple three words: loving, peaceful and kind, does what you are going to post fit in with that theme? A theme like "I create food and feed people to show the kindness of the Lord," would suggest a lot of food, smiling people and kind statements. Would a political post be relevant to this person's theme here? Would cutting down family and friends fit in with this theme? You are right: "no."

Social media should serve you and your purpose. Your social media profile and page should represent you and your theme rather than impulsive messages that you may later regret writing. Take a hold of your accounts and delete things, messages and people that are not supporting you in your belief system. There are many wonderful people out there who don't have the same beliefs as you, and that is okay, provided they are not belittling or cutting you down in public or private forums. Seize your social media and take control.

As a counselor, it was always interesting to hear from my students that the negative social media posts "did not bother them," however the most frequent visitations to my office were about negative social media undermining who these beautiful students really were. These students focused more on what the negative people were saying, rather than what the healthy people were saying. The negative comments weighed more heavily on the students.

A great way to get out of this social media habit is to cut down on the amount of time you spend on social media, have your theme ready to use as a filter, and follow things like scripture posts, nature, animals, food, basically take out the human aspect. When people follow other people they compare themselves to all the pictures, how the person looks, where they go and how many friends they have. Comparing yourself to others is one of the worst strategies you can have in your life. You are "fearfully and wonderfully made." (Psalm 139:14) You can't be someone else. Can you give yourself permission to be the YOU God created for such a time as this? I am sure the world and the supernatural will thank you for it. Take some time and soak in God's theme for you. Is it a short three word reminder, a sentence or a paragraph? Take time and write the theme you have in its working stage in your journal.

Spend time with your journal and reflect.

Speaking of writing things down, journaling is an incredibly powerful life-building tool. When you build time into your daily routine to journal, you're giving yourself time to reflect on the things you've accomplished, the things that upset you, and more. You're giving yourself the ability to fall in love with yourself and know what you want, what has worked for you, how you're living the theme of your life, and how the relationships you have can build you up or even tear you down.

Create time to spend journaling and reflecting on every aspect of your life, your day, and all the feelings that run through your head. This is the time to write it all down and really get familiar with who you are. In this time, pray for the Lord's guidance to reveal His wisdom to you. Get into the Word and write your favorite scriptures down for more inspiration. Write your prayer requests down and reflect back on them from time to time, and I'll bet you find you have not given God the glory or gratitude for some wonderful things He has done in your life. We forget our breakthroughs and miracles. Make sure to remind yourself of what the Good Lord has done for you in a journal or a prayer wall. The prayer wall I have currently has pictures of loved ones, scriptures, affirmations and goals. Try it today.

Remember that you're not alone.

Don't be afraid to ask for the Lord's help at any step along your journey through life. Whether you've just started building the tools to design your life or you've been doing it for years, asking God for His guidance and help in the decisions about relationships, career, and life will bring clarity where you never thought clarity would be possible.

Remember to do as it says in John 14:13,14 "You may ask me for anything in my name, and I will do it." Or in Matthew 7:7, "Ask, and it will be given to you; seek, and you will find; knock, and the door will be opened to you. For everyone who asks receives; he who seeks finds; and to him who knocks, the door will be opened."

Even consider what the Lord shares in Philippians 4;13 "I can do all things through Him who strengthens me" And Isaiah 41:10, "So do not fear, for I am with you; do not be dismayed, for I am your God. I will strengthen you and help you; I will uphold you with my righteous right hand."

In the book of James, the Lord's desire to aid us is communicated, but each person must take initiative and request His help. James 1:5 "If any of you lacks wisdom, he should ask God, who gives generously to all without finding fault, and it will be given to him. But when he asks, he must believe and not doubt because he who doubts is like a wave of the sea, blown and tossed by the wind."

Asking for His guidance and help is one of the benefits of a personal relationship with God. As you follow the Lord, ask for direction, read the Bible and follow your gifts and your theme. Ultimately, seeking Him first will lead you right on His path instead of some impulsive diverged road or imitation of another person's highway to self-actualization.

Grow in your relationship with God.

To be able to truly live in alignment with the gifts and blessings you were born with takes a real deepening of your relationship with His word. Faith and trust are two of the most critical elements to creating a life you love and designing your life.

Yet, both faith and trust are two of the hardest things to embody and live daily as a Christian. First, you have to have trust in God's plan so profoundly that you know it will all work out exactly as it's meant to. Because without first being able to trust God to guide you and lead you on the path He has laid before you, you cannot have the faith required to follow His guidance.

Spending time in prayer and reflection is a great way to grow with God. It creates trust and, in turn, faith as well. And what's the best way to do this?

It's to commit and continue to be comfortable in your relationship with God. After all, trusting in Him is one of the best ways to build the tools for living that you need to start designing your life.

Live your testimony

As a child of God, you have a testimony. You're living proof that you can survive every obstacle, tribulation, and trauma that life throws your way: "You can do all things through Christ who strengthens you." (Philippians 4:13) You made it through the toughest times of loneliness and mental well-being during Covid-19, and you are still alive. You're a living, breathing testament to survival and faith in God's plan for your life. Own that and understand everything that you and God have come through over the past few years.

Take some time to understand all the aspects of your life that make up your testimony. Then, give yourself permission to acknowledge what you've done, everything you've conquered, and how it has impacted your life and made you who you are in the world today. You are appointed to be here at this time and place in the universe. God loves you. Give yourself permission to love yourself as well.

What have you and God come through together?

Write down some of the experiences, traumas, trials, and tribulations that you have gone through in your journey through life and with God. What is it about how you handled those situations that stand out? Where did you feel most like God was carrying you in a time that you never thought you'd have the ability to get through what was going on in your life?

Spend time journaling and reflecting on that question and see what shows up for you. Become present with the feelings that arise from within you.

Next, start keeping records of your testimony and successes to remind yourself of your victories. Your journal can become your greatest uplifter, motivator, and inspiration to continue pushing forward. Because, after all, it is you that you're reading about.

Lastly, you can do something to start designing your life the way you want. Building the career and life of your dreams takes measured action every day of your life. You can't just sit around and think that all the great things you want in life are going to come your way and just fall into your lap. You have to be willing to put the work in, invest the time, and take actionable steps toward your goal every day.

For many people, when they sit back and look at the goals they have for their life, they're instantly stopped from any forward momentum. It's too overwhelming to even know where to begin. Here's a pro-tip, break your goals down into smaller goals and break those smaller goals down into steps. Every part of your goal can be broken down into smaller actionable steps that you can take every day to create forward momentum toward your goal. Don't quit. Keep moving.

You can start creating unstoppable forward momentum toward your goal today. All it takes is creating a routine where you take five actions a day toward your goal. Whatever it is. It could be making a phone call that you've been avoiding to an investor for your idea or drawing out a business plan. Praying for direction, reading the Word, and researching ideas are also great examples of actions you can take each day to move toward accomplishing your goal. Just take five steps a day toward your goal, consistently, and you will see powerful results over time.

Imagine you are a painter and wanted to start a pop-up business at a local art walk in your community. You may have the desire to sell affordable art via greeting cards and larger works of art as well. Brainstorming the different modalities of what you would like to offer your customers could be part of your five actions. The situation we may face today is that we have no tangible paintings or cards to sell, but from today on, you can start producing one greeting card a day and a painting a week. This consistent effort could produce 30 greeting cards and 3-4 paintings to sell. By taking your goals and breaking them down into daily actions, one can relieve anxiety and become validated by the consistent progress he or she is making. Imagine, in just 3 months' time, you could have 90 greeting cards and at least 9 paintings to sell at your pop-up business on the art walk.

CHAPTER THREE

BECOMING COMFORTABLE IN YOUR OWN SKIN

How often have you felt out of place and uncomfortable being who you are in your life? Where does that come from? For so many people and clients that we've worked with at Positive Space, not being comfortable in one's own skin is one of the greatest struggles. Whether it's because of your self-doubts, negative self-talk, or suffocating judgments on who you can be or are able to be, not being comfortable in your own skin can feel like a death sentence. And that's because it is.

Not being able to be your authentic self in everything you do is like the death of your soul. You end up feeling trapped, suffocated, and unhappy in every aspect of your life. So, how do you start living as your authentic self and finally become comfortable in your own skin?

There are a few things that you can do, and God talks about His promises to you when you embrace who you were born to be and why He created you. So, let's dive into those.

Accept who you are in every way.

Things like your negative self-talk can lead you to be unable to accept who you are. Have you ever stood in front of the mirror and judged every spot, wrinkle, fat roll, and blemish on your body? And then take that to make it mean you are unworthy of being loved, enjoying happiness, and more? You're not alone.

It's those self-judgments that prevent you from loving everything about who you are. Now, have you ever noticed people who are living the kind of life that you've always wanted and how they own 100% responsibility for every aspect of their lives, their body, and their relationships? They own it all and take full responsibility for how everything looks because they accept themselves for their faults and strengths together.

When you can see your faults as opportunities to grow and learn and surround yourself with people that complement those faults and weaknesses by celebrating your wins and keeping you account-able, you turn your weaknesses into strengths. And you also lift the people around you in your professional and personal relationships. Yes, we have faults we are working on, but you can't fix them all at the same time. Many people fall away from Jesus Christ because they feel they can't fix themselves and their sin enough to be a Christian. This again is a lie from the pit of Hell. Jesus has already, suffered, died and paid for our sins. All we need to do is receive Him, ask for forgiveness, and have a daily walk with Him. It is a relationship with God, and yours will be completely different from my relationship with God. He's God… He can do that.

Stop judging yourself.

This is one of the most significant points of this section in *Christian Focus In A Blurry World*. So many people spend their entire lives judging everything about themselves. I do it. You do it. We all do. We are all our own worst enemies, the most vocal critics, and the only person in our lives that can stop us from doing what we want to do.

It's true. When you embrace everything about who you are and the blessings you were born to share with the world, life has a way of conspiring on your behalf. The only real pathway to stop judging yourself is to accept who you are. Once you stop the harsh judgments and discover acceptance, you can actually see the ways to learn and grow. We're all learning every day and spending time reading books, taking classes, or other ways to build and develop your interpersonal relationship skills, grow closer with God, and learn to master the skills needed to create a life you love. Never stop doing this and give yourself permission to be the wonderful person that our Lord created.

The more you understand about your weaknesses, the more you can see where you want to change. As you work to develop your weaknesses, it's quite possible to turn those around into strengths. Start by making the commitment to yourself to make small changes in your life.

Just like your goals, if you focus on the bigger picture the entire time, it will just overwhelm you to the point that you'll remain stuck where you're at—growing means taking it one small thing at a time. You can't change everything all at once. It's impossible. And trying to do so is unhealthy. Think of growth like an onion. You have to peel one layer back, and when you do, there's a new one that you discover, and within that layer, there are other things that you now want to work on and develop. It's a process. Be patient with the process and continuously focus on God's complete and whole love for you. You are whole. You are whole today because Jesus was broken on the cross making you whole. Take a few minutes, put your hand over your heart and say: "I am whole, I am whole, I am whole." Reflect on this.

Remember that God loves you as you are.

This seems to be something that so many people forget. We get so caught up in the ways of the world, social media, and the way we're "supposed to be," that we forget that only through our relationship with Jesus Christ can we experience God's everlasting and unconditional love for us exactly as we are. "Who shall separate us from the love of Christ? Shall trouble or hardship or persecution or famine or nakedness or danger or sword? No, in all these things, we are more than conquerors through him who loved us. For I am convinced that neither death nor life, neither angels nor demons, neither the present nor the future, nor any powers, neither height nor depth, nor anything else in all creation, will be able to separate us from the love of God, this is in Christ Jesus our Lord." (Romans 8:35; 37-39)

And when you feel like you've done wrong, His forgiveness already awaits you. Do you want to see evidence of His love for you and the forgiveness that awaits?

Psalm 103:12 "as far as the east is from the west, so far has he removed our transgressions from us."

Micah 7:19 "You will again have compassion on us; you will tread our sins underfoot and hurl all our iniquities into the depths of the sea."

1 John 1:9 "If we confess our sins, he is faithful and just and will forgive us our sins and purify us from all unrighteousness."

All of these verses above are great examples of God's unconditional love for you that's found through His son Jesus Christ.

The 25% Rule

What do we mean by this? We're talking about understanding that not everyone is going to think the same way that you do, believe in the same things you do, or have the same approach to life that you do. And that's okay. It's essential to understand this because when you're living with a Jesus focused mindset and participating in this massive game in life, you're going to offend people.

You can't please everyone, and you're never going to. So, it's essential to understand that fact now as you're working to make changes in your life. People can be easily offended. That's just how it goes. Something incredibly important to keep in mind is that people are deathly afraid and uncomfortable about things and people they don't understand.

There is a rule of 25%. It's a proven fact that 25% of all the people you meet will not like you and about 25% of people may like you at first and then grow to dislike you. The third component to this is 25% of people may not like you at first and then eventually begin to like you. 25% of people you meet will gravitate to you and like you for who you are. If you look at the data, just by being your true self, 25% of people will like you in your own skin and 50% of people are in and out of liking you. The negative crowd, who will not like you no matter what you do, is a waste of time to pursue. I have pursued relationships with these negative 25%, and it always ended in rejection. I got in my own way by transforming my behavior, my talk and even my look to be like theirs in the hope that they would accept me. My desire and effort to morph into the negative 25% was fruitless, and I felt like a different person than how I feel now comfortable in my own skin. (Appendix I)

One of the most impactful mindsets you can adopt in your life is knowing that you're going to offend people, some people will not like you and that is okay. The sooner you accept this, the easier life is going to be and the sooner you can stop trying to fit into other people's idealistic mold of you. It's essential to your survival in those times to understand that it doesn't concern you. Their judgments, fears, and doubts aren't yours, and they don't impact your ability to live your fullest life as your true authentic self.

If they can't wrap their head around you or why you think and act the way you do, they're going to be scared of how it makes them feel. Remember that some people may get scared in a positive way and be propelled to another level by the energy and hope you bring. Understanding the 25% Rule helps you to understand and accept that you can't please everyone. Having this unrealistic expectation that everyone will love you will only leave you depressed when you can't figure out why people are not attracted to you. Be yourself and what the Good Lord called you to be—you.

God desires you to be a space for love, kindness, grace, and understanding to people, whether they like you or not. By being a space for all of those things, you're giving people the ability to step into that same space with you. When you give people the ability to show up in that kind of space that you are modeling for them, more often than not, they will. Leading a life boldly in Christ will attract the right people and tribe to you.

Be a good steward.

That's where we're going with this. By being that Positive Space for others, you're naturally a good steward for the people you love, the people who love you, and even those who don't like you. It's this approach to life that is needed to survive and to create a life you love.

It's where your authentic self and purpose will show up in so many ways. It's what God did for you before you were even created.

He sent his Son to die on the cross for our sins so we could be saved and enjoy life after death in Heaven. And if you've received Jesus as your personal Lord and Savior, you have the ability to tap into a supernatural power by calling on the name of Jesus.

What can this do for you?

Well, when you have done all you can and submit to surrendering your cares to the Lord, you have the peace that surpasses all understanding. (Philippians 4:7) This is peace of mind, body, and spirit that no amount of money can buy. You literally are surrendering to His plan for your life. When you pray and ask God for the life you want and to guide you, you don't ever have to ask again. He hears your prayer and will see to it that your pathway is shown to you when you're ready and, He will set you up for success every step of the way. "For I know the plans I have for you," declares the Lord, "plans to prosper you and not to harm you, plans to give you hope and a future." (Jeremiah 29:11)

Surrendering your space to Almighty God will allow the heavens to be opened over you and for the devourers to be rebuked. Here at Positive Space, we sincerely believe that when you are a Jesus Follower, you have a supernatural space. Being a good steward of relationships and money, in Jesus' Mighty name will gain you this special Positive Space that no weapon formed against you shall prosper. (Isaiah 54:11)

The two verses that are key to the philosophy of keeping your Positive Space are found in Malachai: "And I will rebuke the devourer for your sake, and he shall not destroy the fruits of your ground; neither shall your vine cast her fruit before the time in the field, saith the Lord of hosts." (Malachi 3:11 KJV) The second verse relates to dealing with money, "Bring ye all the tithes into the storehouse, that there may be meat in the mine house, and prove me now herewith, saith the Lord of hosts, if I will not open you the windows of heaven, and pour you out a blessing, that there shall not be room enough to receive it" (Malachai 3:10 KJV) Amen to this. The Lord will keep the space over your land, home and people blessed and the devourer will be rebuked over your territory. Proclaim this truth over your life: the heavens are open and the devourer is rebuked.

Life is messy!

When we are born into this world, it is messy. If you really think about it, we are born in blood and are coming out of a small canal being squeezed and bumped around. Why then do we expect that we won't be bumping each other on this planet, in our country, in our churches? It is a misconception that in finding a church the people will all be wonderful, loving and ready to greet you. It is said that when you're looking for a perfect church and you find it, don't join it because you will ruin it. There is no church that has a perfect culture. God has His intention on fellowship: "and let us consider one another to provoke unto love and to good works: not forsaking the assembling of ourselves together, as the manner of some is; but exhorting one another: and so much the more, as ye see the day approaching." (Hebrews 10:24, 25 KJV)

The focus on fellowship and encouraging each other, especially in the end days, is the intended purpose of the church. The NIV version states: "And let us consider how we may spur one another on toward love and good deeds, not giving up meeting together, as some are in the habit of doing, but encouraging one another and all the more as you see the Day approaching." (Hebrews 10:24, 25 NIV) Even though we may be frustrated with different relationships or people that refuse to treat us with respect or kindness in the church, we are still called to fellowship. God calls us to fellowship with each other to encourage us to do good, especially when approaching the Day.

There will be many things that happen that make you uncomfortable, things that leave you shaken and bruised.

Life is messy no matter how you're living it. But there are things that you can do to discover the peace and grace you need to survive it all.

Understand that offenses happen.

As we've already established, people may offend you. You also have the potential to offend others at the game you're playing in life. They're not going to understand why you do the things you do and what for. They're going to be offended by your accomplishments, your testimony, and by your belief in God. But that doesn't mean that you just stop in your tracks and let their judgments and offenses cause you to give up on creating a powerful life in Christ Jesus that you love.

It's just part of living a great life on fire for God and filled with passion and purpose that creates unstoppable momentum. Remember that God says: "You did not choose me, but I chose you and appointed you to go and bear fruit fruit that will last. Then the Father will give you whatever you ask in my name. This is my command: Love each other." (John 15:16) You must keep your momentum and your theme in the front of your mind rather than let people suck the joy out of your journey in Christ.

If you are not living your chosen theme in your life, it is highly doubtful you will feel like you are comfortable in your own skin. I remember trying to fit in with a certain crowd of employees at a school that I worked at. No matter how I tried to be liked or respected by them, it did not work. I changed my theme to fit the employees I wanted to like me. My theme and comfort in my own skin was void. The biggest blessing you can have is living your own theme knowing that you are true to God and authentically comfortable in your own skin.

You cannot please everyone, and the moment you stop trying, you can discover a freedom of living you never thought possible. Do you constantly feel like you have to make everyone else happy? Do you feel like whatever you do for others is never good enough? Or never what they wanted in the first place? Do you feel rejected?

You're not alone. So many of my clients struggle with trying to stay on top of everyone else's needs, so much so that they forget about their own. Know that you can't please everyone and that you're going to offend people when you set healthy boundaries for yourself. The people that want you to be prompted to "do something" for them will be the most shocked and offended by you. And own that. Do what God has called you to do, not what you perceive other people want from you.

Have realistic goals for yourself and the relationships you are in. Are there any boundaries in your relationships that you need to revise? Are there conversations that you need to have to enable an agreement on new boundaries that will allow you to be you in your own skin? Take a few moments to journal and meditate on John 15:16 for at least 5 minutes.

What about when you're being attacked?

Always remember that Jesus has got you. When you're offending people by living your big life, there are going to be some hurt feelings and egos along the way. And in turn, those hurt feelings and egos are going to lash out and attack you.

That's what happens. Living a big life makes people uncomfortable, and when you're at your highest and especially on the verge of your greatness, that's when the devil will come after you. He never wants you to have the things he knows will spread God's love throughout the world. So he uses others to tear you down and put obstacles in your way.

Being attacked isn't something that you have to go through on your own. However, if everyone and everything around you is attacking you, that's when you pray to the Lord and ask Jesus to intercede on your behalf. Live that Proverbs 3:5 Mindset and He will make your path straight. Ask Jesus to intercede in your situation, your family, your home and your place of work.

This works in ways you can never imagine until you see it up close and personal for yourself. So, take the time to pray in the name of Jesus, that the evil that's attacking you be exposed for what it is and trust completely in Him.

If it happens to be a fellow follower of Christ, pray for God to intervene and continue to trust in His plan and guidance as you watch for your miracle. It will come. Only God can truly transform the hearts of man. Trust that when you're living in tune with His blessings, passion, and purpose, He will take care of your every step. It's the Proverbs 3:5 Mindset friend.

Fight, flee, or flexibility?

When you are being attacked, there are three strategies at your disposal. You can choose to fight it. If you choose to fight it, pray first. Is this the battle you were meant to fight? Is this something you are willing to fight for and possibly lose someone close to you over? Does this fight fit in with Biblical principles or is it just a reaction without thought and Biblical wisdom?

You can always choose to flee and escape from an uncomfortable situation or tempting fight. Your last option is to choose to be flexible. Is this a subject that can be modified or is there a healthy compromise that can ensue? Can you build upon others' ideas? Before you choose to fight everything around you, analyze the cost of your energy, possible relationship fallout, and any creative way to solve your current situation. If you are ever physically attacked, defend yourself and get help immediately.

So, where do we go from here?

Transforming your life with God requires trust and faith. But it also requires your ability to transform your mindset. If you can't change the MP3 or playlist playing in your head from negatively charged energy, how can you do the great things you were created for?

If you aim at nothing, you'll get nothing. Remember that your life is a journey. Taking the approach to life of simply going where it takes you is great, except that you have little to no say on where life and the people in it will take you. You're literally at the mercy of the universe and others' whims to guide who you are, what you do, and what you can be. That's an incredibly powerless existence, isn't it?

Living your greatest life filled with light and love and sharing your gifts with the world requires you to be an active member of the world. It also means you have a say about what your life looks like. God created you to be a light for the world and to bless us all with your gifts. "You are the light of the world. A town built on a hill cannot be hidden, neither do people light a lamp and put it under a bowl. Instead, they put it on its stand, and it gives light to everyone in the house. In the same way, let your light shine before others, that they may see your good deeds and glorify your Father in heaven." (Matthew 5:14-16)

What are these gifts? How can you tap into them and create a life where you're sharing your gifts with the world with everything you do?

That's exactly what we're about to discover as we work through this book! So, are you ready to take control of your life and create an unstoppable existence that's filled with all the great things you've always wanted?

Keep reading to find out!

CHAPTER FOUR

GET OFF YOUR ASSETS AND CONQUER YOUR DREAMS!

Creating anything worth having in life requires time, effort, and commitment to something amazing. And now that you're learning how to stop being held back by your fears and self-doubts, it's time to get off your ass-ets and start creating your own real-life waking dream.

If you could have anything you've ever wanted, what would it be? If you could have the job of your dreams, what would it look like? If you could live anywhere in the world, where would you live? All of these questions have only one solution to get you where you want to be…they require purposeful action every day.

There are so many people that we've worked with in the past who feel like life should just give them the things that they want. As if they're just destined for greatness, but they don't have to do anything to get it. It's not about earning, but life and God have a funny way of blessing you with the things you've dreamed of having, but only once you've done the work to become the person who's ready to bear the burden that comes with greatness and success.

In a way, putting in the work to become the person you were born to be involves becoming a believer who embodies the love of God in everything he or she does, and someone that understands that all of our blessings are not for us but for others, and to leave this world a better place than how we found it. It's only then you get the blessings you've always wanted.

God tests you and puts you through Hell, if you will, so that He can chisel away at the clay that is your soul, spirit, and character to mold you into the woman or man you were born to be. Denying that or thinking that you should just be given all of that isn't living. It's laziness. I always look at being lazy and completely out of tune with God's will as *taking another lap around the desert.*

Fear will cause you to avoid reality, a response that will destroy your richest dreams in life, just like it did when God made a generation of people wander in the desert because they were too afraid to conquer the promised land. We read in the Old Testament, "Then I said to you, 'you have reached the hill country of the Amorites, which the Lord our God is giving us. See, the Lord your God has given you the land. Go up and take possession of it as the Lord, the God of your ancestors, told you. Do not be afraid; do not be discouraged.'" (Deuteronomy 1:20, 21)

Notice God had instructed them to have no fear and trust Him. The Israelites asked Moses to send spies to the promised land to get a report and more information on those they would be invading. This was a delay because they did not have the courage to follow the Lord's command, they were in fact very afraid and would rather take another *lap around the desert.*

Sometimes people don't move because they are comfortable doing what they have always done, some people don't know what to do to get moving, and some people are paralyzed with fear, like Moses' people.

The report from the spies about the land was indeed good. The Israelites then decided to complain about God and get really comfortable with *taking another lap around the desert.*

The Israelites started to create new fears by saying: "The people are stronger and taller than we are; the cities are large, with walls up to the sky. We even saw the Anakites there." (Deuteronomy 1:28) Caleb had tried to keep the Israelites moving toward God's plan, "Then Caleb silenced the people before Moses and said, 'We should go up and take possession of the land, for we can certainly do it.'" (Numbers 13:30) Moses also told the Israelites: "Do not be terrified; do not be afraid of them. The Lord your God, who is going before you, will fight for you, as he did for you in Egypt, before your very eyes, and in the wilderness. There you saw how the Lord your God carried you, as a father carries his son, all the way you went until you reached this place." (Deuteronomy 1:29-31)

The Israelites did not trust in God and decided to be paralyzed by their own fear and even blamed God out of their own fear. The Lord decided that He would not allow a whole generation to enter into the land He promised them, "No one from this evil generation shall see the good land I swore to give your ancestors, except Caleb son of Jephunneh. He will see it, and I will give him and his descendants the land he set his feet on, because he followed the Lord wholeheartedly." (Deuteronomy 1:35-36) This generation would not trust God and move to claim their land, as a result they had to spend 40 years wandering in the desert, "one for each of the forty days you explored the land." (Numbers 14:34)

How many laps do you want to take in the desert? Are you willing to take your eyes off of God's plan for your life and miss your promised land? To truly conquer your dreams and prayers, you have to get up, move, take measured and strategic action each and every day—you can't get to where you want to be otherwise. Take some time to identify delays in your life created by fears, laziness, inaction, and clinging to what is a comfortable zone for you. What held you back? What mindset could you have embraced to reach your dreams, prayers, and goals at those times? Take time to journal and reflect for at least 5 minutes.

How can you take action every day?

Getting off your ass-ets starts with something as simple as building physical activities into your daily routine for as little as 30 minutes a day. Even if you don't like exercise, it has many benefits to your mindset and can transform your productivity and get you moving. Motion is lotion for your body. When you physically move, such as practicing flexibility, stamina, and muscle strength, some of the myths and fears in your mind start to melt away.

Let's look at six ways that exercising every day can supercharge your productivity:

Exercise keeps you alert and focused.
Exercise increases the blood flow to your brain, and naturally, that just sharpens your awareness. A study by Jim McKenna from the University of Bristol showed that work performance was higher, time management was better, and mental sharpness was also improved after exercise[1].

Exercise kicks up your energy levels.
Let's be honest, there are days, especially if you've never really been active, when the last thing you want to do, either early in the morning or at the end of a long workday, is any kind of physical activity. Who has the energy to function at that level all the time? It sounds counterintuitive but choosing to exercise, no matter what time of

---

[1]   Coulson J.C., McKenna J., Field M. "Exercising at work and self reported work performance." International Journal of Workplace Health Management. 2008. 1:3, pp.176-197. http://dx.doi.org/10.1108/17538350810926534

day, can provide you with the energy boost you need. "It's the paradox of exercise, to get energy, you have to expend some."[2]

Exercise improves brain function.
According to John Medina, author of Brain Rules, physically active people score better on cognitive tests than people living a sedentary lifestyle. In addition, in a clinical trial run by the Body-Brain Performance Institute associated with Swinburne's University and Brain Sciences Institute, there was a clear link between physical fitness, brain function, and reduced stress levels at work. So, the increased blood flow to your brain that comes with exercise naturally helps your cognitive function no matter what you're doing with your life and career.

Exercise can spark a breakthrough idea.
Are you stuck on an idea? Do you feel like you've just stalled out? Or maybe you're wrestling with the same problem for most of the workday? Then, get outside and go take a walk. A study in the Journal of Experimental Psychology demonstrated that walking indoors and outdoors triggered a burst in creative thinking, with the average creative output rising 60 percent when a person was walking. You never know what can come to you when you're soaking in God's creations. A walk outside when you're stuck on an idea is like spending time in prayer with the Lord, and when you're quiet like that, He will converse with you.

Exercise helps you find your optimal work-life balance.
Think that an after-work workout session is just another item to cross off your to-do list? Think again. In an article in the Harvard Business Review, people who managed to stick with their regular exercise routine experienced less trouble finding an optimal work-life balance, possibly because structured activity helped them become better at time management and more confident in their ability to pull off the demands of both work and home.

---

[2] Ibid.

Exercise helps you learn how to work through discomfort.
No matter how long you've exercised regularly, there are days you wake up or finish work and don't feel at all like you want to hit the gym or go for that walk. And that's where regular exercise can teach you to work through discomfort. The key is to change your script around working out. When that voice in your mind tells you to skip exercising for the day, you have to remember how you feel after spending an hour in the gym. Or even remind yourself how much you regret not going whenever you skip days. Or even that being healthy is part of serving those you love because you're at the top of your game. It's because of this that you can learn to work through discomfort and negative self-talk by focusing on incorporating 30 minutes of exercise into your daily routine.

How you can incorporate exercise into your life today

- Walk to the *second*-closest coffee shop in the morning for your coffee, take the stairs instead of the elevator, and park as far from the front door as possible. Commit to doing this once in the next week.
- Set a 'move your legs' timer. Get up and walk around your office, up and down the hallways, or around the building for 10 minutes. It does not take much to reap the rewards of exercise. Commit to doing this three times in the next week.
- Find an exercise buddy. This person, either in person or online, will serve as your accountability partner and cheerleader as you incorporate exercise into your life.
- Get a Fitbit or an Apple iwatch to monitor your daily steps and set new goals for yourself every week.
- Make it fun!

So now that you're taking steps to incorporate regular movement and activity as part of creating measured action every day... what's next?

It's time to learn your ABCs!

No, we're not going back to kindergarten, we promise! What we mean by learning your ABCs is to Always Be Creating!

Having taken on moving every day, that forward momentum has to transition into something else in your professional life. So while exercise helps keep you focused and on track, for your career, you have to have the same kind of forward motion.

And to get that kind of forward motion needed, you have to Always Be Creating. Every part of you was created. Your past helped define and create who you are in the world today. The future that you're **creating** is just that—a creation.

And your present—right now, at this moment—you have the power to create and transform with God because He is the Creator of you and your gifts. So by taking time to focus on always creating something, you are using those gifts, combined with the lessons learned from your past, and working to create a future that you love.

You have the gifts and talents, and He wants you to use them to create something meaningful in the world. That's where discovering your purpose using the gifts God blessed you with comes into play.

So, how do you find your purpose and unlock your best life? There's no better way to do that than to equip yourself with the tools you need to tap into and discover your purpose. Because at Positive Space, we want you to succeed and understand that the best way to predict your future is to keep moving and create it with God.

That's why we've put together 12 quick steps to start finding your purpose today.

Step One: Receive Jesus Christ as your Lord and Savior today

Jesus Christ is not just a person. He is God in human form, the Son Of God. Jesus came to save us from guilt, shame and condemnation. This is a really huge concept to wrap your mind around, but it is Truth. Jesus lived on earth, taught, created miracles, was murdered, and then rose from the dead.

These are some Old Testament prophecies that have been fulfilled in the New Testament in Jesus Christ:[3]

- Isaiah 7:14 predicts Immanuel will be born of a virgin, fulfilled in Luke 1:35
- Micah5:2 discusses the Christ will be born in Bethlehem, fulfilled in Matthew 2:4-6
- Isaiah 53:3 describes that He would be despised and rejected, fulfilled in Luke 4: 28,29
- Zechariah 11:12–13 describes 30 pieces of silver that were valued and thrown in the potters house, fulfilled in Matthew 27:6-10
- Exodus 12:46 states no bones of Jesus were broken just as in the sacrificed holy lamb, fulfilled John19:31-36
- Psalm 22:16 the piercing of hands and feet, fulfilled in John 19:36–37

Prophesy that was fulfilled in Christ's genealogy, holy life, death and resurrection are found all over the Old Testament, and fulfilled in the New Testament.

Take some time to pray right now and connect with God. Is it time for you to receive Jesus in your heart? Is it time to renew your heart for Jesus? Say this simple prayer right now and receive Jesus as your personal Lord and Savior.

"Jesus, I have sinned. I feel guilty every day and I want to surrender my guilt and shame to you. Please take my sins and wipe them away. I am sorry for sinning against You. Jesus, I believe you are the Son of God and that you died for me on the cross to restore me to the Father. I trust in You Lord. I thank you for coming into my heart and giving me your Holy Spirit to guide me. In Jesus' name I pray, Amen."

---

[3]   https://www.jesusfilm.org/blog-and-stories/old-testament-prophecies.html

You may feel the need to *renew* your heart and commitment to Jesus right now. He knows you better than you know yourself. He has made you a new creature. Let's renew our hearts in Jesus' name right now.

"Lord, I know that I have sinned against you and I want to renew my commitment to you. I am sorry for my sin, please wipe it out. I release any guilt, shame and condemnation to you Lord, right now. Thank you for loving me. Thank you that I am yours and no weapon formed against me shall prosper. Thank you for living in me."

If you have said either of these prayers, or even something similar to these prayers, you are a Jesus Follower. Following Jesus is the most critical path to finding your purpose in life, and it is exciting to see the Lord work in your life. As I said earlier in this book, I can give you all the strategies and counseling plans I have and all of it is nothing without Jesus Christ, The Son Of The Living God.

You now have the gift of the Holy Spirit, the gift of Eternal Life, the gift of justification, and the gift of forgiveness, because God did this for you through His one and only Son. Follow the rest of these steps to cultivate a purposeful, exciting and fulfilling life in Christ.

Step Two: Create a personal vision statement, your theme

By creating a personal vision statement, you can help manage stress and find balance in your life. This directly correlates to defining the theme of your life. Your personal vision statement serves as a roadmap to help guide you toward your purpose by identifying your core values and establishing what's important to you. As we discussed, having a simple three word purpose or sentence that you can easily remember will help you filter things out of your space that are not serving you or God.

A purpose statement creates a space for you to make decisions that are aligned with your values and helps keep you motivated as you work toward your personal goals. Ever notice how tempted you are to respond in anger to a negative comment towards you or another person you care about? Use your purpose statement to clear your mind before responding to any rubbish that humans are trying to throw at you. Before you respond 1) pray, 2) use your purpose statement to filter what you will respond to the comment and 3) your purpose statement may take away your need to respond. If my purpose statement is "creating a positive space for people to connect and find Jesus," maybe responding in anger does not fit. The Lord may be prompting you to "be still and know He is God," or reduce the amount of time you are allocating to a negative person as a part of keeping your healthy boundaries. (Psalm 46:10)

Step Three: Read the Bible daily, the source for hearing the Master's voice

As humans in the digital age, we're surrounded by voices, and they're not always good. So it's essential to be able to decipher God's voice from among the constant barrage of noise and voices from the outside world.

Whether you're spending time constantly scrolling through your phone on social media, talking with your loved ones, or watching the news, if you can't hear your own voice, how do you know what life you want to live?

Chances are, you don't. You have to be able to bring peace and silence to your life and listen to God's voice in your life. So put down the phone, turn off the TV, check out from the digital distractions and spend time in the Word. Spend time reading the Bible every day, a new verse, a Psalm, or a whole book of the Bible. These are the Lord's **B**asic **I**nstructions **B**efore **L**eaving **E**arth and you can hear from the Lord directly through the Bible. The more you do this, the easier it is to know what's right for your life and whether you're on the right path, because you are listening to God now, not the world.

Step Four: Practice prayer without ceasing

God wants to hear from you. He desires that you talk to him all day and that connection grows stronger and yields more signs and miracles, if you allow yourself to humble yourself and simply pray.

"…if my people, who are called by my name, will humble themselves and pray and seek my face and turn from their wicked ways, then I will hear from heaven, and I will forgive their sin and will heal their land." (2 Chronicles 7:14) We are told to pray without ceasing, meaning, pray at work, school, before your meals, when you are sad, angry, depressed, confused, frustrated at home, planing your life, when you are happy and when you are grateful. Sometimes we forget that praying can be a simple "I love you" to God or a thankful shout of praise!

Include God in all parts of your life and it becomes very natural and easy to talk to God. Do you know when the best time to pray is? It's when you don't feel like praying. When you feel embarrassed, ashamed or sad about something and you "don't want to bother him," this is not serving your purpose or being transparent with God. Remember, He already knows you. He is your personal Lord and Savior. God did not tell you to get perfect before praying to Him. He expects you to talk to him at all times, because you are developing your relationship with Him. Give yourself permission to cry out to him and feel your feelings. He commands you to do this because He knows you can't handle life on your own.

Step Five: Practice gratitude

Focusing on gratitude in your life can help you have a crystal-clear vision of your purpose. You'll start and end your day in the space of thankfulness for everything and everyone around you. Cultivating gratitude helps make you more generous and leads to acts of kindness being a part of your inner fiber. This approach to life actually contributes to helping you feel a sense of purpose in every aspect of your life.

If you've never brought the practice of gratitude into your life before, one of the best ways to get started is by taking time to write down three to five things that you feel grateful for first thing in the morning or at night before you go to bed. Thank God for these wonderful things by holding and feeling love for Him as you communicate your gratitude for at least 5 minutes. "Rejoice always, pray continually, give thanks in all circumstances; for this is God's will for you in Christ Jesus." (1 Thessalonians 5:16)

"Give thanks to the Lord, for He is good; his love endures forever." (Psalm 107:1)

Step Six: Offer the sacrifice of praise

There are times when you are not going to feel happy or even feel like you deserve to be happy. If you have ever felt like praise and worship is not what you want to do, it is okay. Offer God the "sacrifice of praise." (Hebrews 13:15,16) There are going to be times you don't feel worthy to praise Him or may possibly even feel like you don't have the energy to praise Him. May I suggest starting with a smile? Research suggests that smiling, even if it is not sincere, actually boosts your mood, your immune system and relieves stress.[4] When God requires you to offer the sacrifice of praise, this will also boost your mood and allow you to connect with the Lord and feel His presence.

Start with a smile, turn on your favorite worship playlist and sing to Him a song of praise. Let all your worries and tension be surrendered to God and take time to change and shift any negative thoughts, pain or resentment away from you. God is big enough to carry your burdens. God is big enough to snap you out of your self-defeating thoughts.

Take your arms, reach them to the heavens, sing, speak His praises or speak in tongues. Make big movements, walk around your home proclaiming how good our Lord is for at least five minutes and I

---

[4]   https://www.verywellmind.com/top-reasons-to-smile-every-day-2223755

know you will feel the benefits of offering praise, even when you don't feel like doing it.[5] Research shows that this kind of distraction from negative emotions actually serves as a great coping tool to prevent anxiety and depression. You can use distraction methods to cope with very intense emotions rather than running to temporary fixes like alcohol and other drugs. Distraction is considered a very healthy way to cope with distressing emotions. There have been many times that I have wanted to turn to temporary fixes such as comfort food or bingeing out on Amazon or Netflix movies for hours. Using worship and praise has really fixed my mental mood, alleviates stress, and has kept my attention and focus on God rather than the blur of emotions I am feeling at that moment.

Try this playlist

- Surrounded (Fight My Battles), Michael W. Smith
- Raise a Hallelujah, Bethel Music, Jonathan David Helser & Melissa Helser
- Way Maker, Performed By Leeland
- Voice Of Truth, Casting Crowns
- Here As In Heaven, Elevation Worship
- Help, Erica Campbell
- Won't He Do It, Koryn Hawthorne
- Hillsong
- Salvador
- Chris Tomlin

Step Seven: Volunteer your talent and time

Everyone has a cause that they feel passionately about. Maybe you have strong feelings about animal welfare, the environment, social justice, or the church body you are with. (1 Corinthians 12:12) Whatever you're passionate about in the world and want to help create change in, fighting for a cause helps tie together many of the tips above, including:

---

[5] https://www.verywellmind.com/coping-with-emotions-with-distraction-2797606

- Giving back
- Forming part of a community
- Doing something you're passionate about
- Surrounding yourself with people who inspire you
- Working as a part of the body of Christ (Romans 12:4,5)

Whatever you're passionate about, get involved today and see how easy it is to find more purpose in your life. Giving back enhances your sense of meaning and purpose in life, because serving others is part of sharing the love of Christ with the world. When you take time to serve others, you're creating a deep connection with them and experiencing their love as you share yours. You're helping others and helping yourself at the same time. This is where you will find your highest fulfillment.

Try to find ways to be of service to others, whether it's volunteering in your local community, or donating money or your skills to a cause that resonates with you. You can even try spreading a little happiness by performing random acts of kindness. RAK's are quick, fun and positivity boosting for your mind and spirit.

Step Eight: Give back with your finances
I joyfully give my time, talent and tithe. Yes, giving is a crucial component to this heavenly protection and blessing and this is the reason why being a good steward of your money, time and talents are so important. The Lord sees what you are doing. The more you communicate to Him and connect with the Bible the more you have that intimate relationship with God and the confidence that is found there. Second guessing your tithe over and over takes away from the security of the relationship that you will find in Jesus Christ.

People around you will have many different goals and relationships with money and giving, and some do not give it at all. Giving releases an instantaneous joy, especially when you reflect on what you have given and the impact it has had on another human beings. The Lord loves to bless and give, "Give, and it will be given to you. A good measure, pressed down, shaken together and running over, will be poured into your lap. For with the measure you use, it will be measured to you." (Luke 6:38) Paul testifies: "Remember this: Whoever sows sparingly will also reap sparingly, and whoever sows generously will also reap generously. Each of you should give what you have decided in your heart to give, not reluctantly or under compulsion, for God loves a cheerful giver. And God is able to bless you abundantly, so that in all things at all times, having all that you need, you will abound in every good work." (2 Corinthians 9:6-8) Through these financial promises we have seen breakthroughs. God never fails you in His promises and He loves a cheerful giver.

Step Nine: Become part of a church community

Your purpose is all about being and feeling connected to others. So when you become an active member of a Bible believing church, it can naturally lead to creating a greater sense of purpose in your life. When you create a fellowship with other believers, you'll discover that many others out there want to experience you and share in your goals to get closer to Christ, the Son of the Living God. As the children of the Most High God, we can encourage each other and inspire one another; "And let us consider how we may spur one another on toward love and good deeds, not giving up meeting together, as some are in the habit of doing, but encouraging one another and all the more as you see the Day approaching." (Hebrews 10:24, 25)

You are who you surround yourself with. If you're spending all of your time with people who are angry at the world and feel like everyone and everything is out to get them, guess what approach and mindset you're going to have about life? The same kind of mindset that they have. Having a healthy church family will give you great worship, Bible based messages, and fellowship opportunities.

Take time to examine the relationships you have with your colleagues, family, and friends, and look at who you're spending your time with regularly. Make sure that you're surrounding yourself with people who are up to big things in life, that are living a life through inspired action, and support and lift up your dreams too.

Step Ten: Practice self-acceptance

Realize and accept your limitations. This type of approach to your life helps you be kinder to yourself when things go wrong. It creates a natural blockade in your brain to that negative self-tape or MP3 that loves to kick in and tear you down when you fail. The same one that prevents you from getting back up right away. Understand that you're going to make mistakes, but instead of beating yourself up about it when you fail, take a step back, look for the lesson, and create an opportunity to find growth.

Living with self-compassion helps you become more self-aware and self-accepting. When you're able to accept all of yourself, you're more likely to give the best of yourself in everything you do.

Step Eleven: Take time for self-care

Self-care comes in many forms. But remember that your version of self-care is completely unique to you. Perhaps you like walking by the ocean, practicing some deep breathing, or journaling out your difficult emotions.

But why is self-care important? Because when your brain is relaxed, you're at your most creative. You cannot serve others or unlock your full potential when you're literally battling at war against yourself. Get out of your own way.

Have you ever noticed that some of your best ideas come when you're in the shower? That's because your mind is more open and receptive to the flow of ideas than when you're forcing yourself to think.

Step Twelve: Turn your pain into purpose.

Everyone faces struggles in life, and overcoming these challenges helps form who you will become and gives you your unique strengths and perspectives.

No matter where you're at in your life, you will find yourself asking for help when you're struggling to overcome a significant life change. These times in our lives allow us to discover our purpose by helping others face the same struggles that we have learned to overcome.

As you're helping others through challenges, you may discover that you love helping others discover their greatness, passions, and purpose. Or you may discover that creating art, writing, or even music enables you to make an impact in the lives of others and inspire them through your creations. Whatever the case may be, all of those types of arts and careers that come with them are all influenced directly by the pain you've experienced in your past. Creation is the art of transforming your pain into purpose. During the years of 2000-2001, I faced incredible anger and I turned that energy into a complete Christian Music CD called "Don't Step On Me." Creating this CD allowed me to focus on Christ and something other than my pain and anger. Instead of creating negative actions, I produced a musical compilation for my God.

Christian Trance

Christian Jazz & Blues

How you transform your pain into purpose is up to you. God is loving and is healing you on your purpose journey, "He heals the brokenhearted and binds up their wounds." (Psalm 147:3)

All of these twelve steps are great ways to tap into and discover your purpose in life. So start practicing them today and see how quickly you can create a life you love!

We've covered your purpose. Do you have an idea of what your purpose in life is? You may even have a thousand different thoughts running through your head about what to do. So, before continuing on to the next chapter, take some time to reflect and journal about your purpose. Don't be afraid to be honest with yourself about where you're succeeding, where you're failing, and the things that you can start to build into your daily routine to create long-term growth. At Positive Space, we encourage daily prayer and Bible reading to be part of your daily actions for the best growth results. Remember, we are looking for inspired action to create our future.

What are some things that you're grateful for? Writing these things down along with your reflections on each chapter of *Christian Focus In A Blurry World* will help you sort through your inner dialogue and sift out the negativity and noise. This way, you can find clarity around things you may have never thought you would get clarity over. After all, that's what this book is designed to do.

Ready to move on? In the following few sections, we're going to discuss people, how to handle them, how to listen to them, and even how to communicate better so that you're making the most of your time as well as honoring your truth and voice in the world.

CHAPTER FIVE

PEOPLE WILL TELL YOU WHO THEY ARE... LISTEN TO THEM! NOT SURE HOW? WE CAN HELP!

You know that old adage that people will tell you exactly who they are if you listen closely, and if you don't listen long enough, they'll end up showing you? Well, that old adage is one of the most significant truths in our lives.

People will tell you exactly who they are, but are you able to actually be present long enough to listen? Are you so caught up in your own stresses, worries, and fears, desperately waiting for help or just to be heard, that you can't see the toxic people for who they really are, even when they're showing you all day, every day, exactly how bad for you they are?

Whether you have developed an accurate toxic person radar yet or not, this next section of *Christian Focus In A Blurry World* will guide you through a deep and comprehensive dive into some of the most effective ways to weed out the people that may be preventing you from fulfilling your dreams or are sidetracking God's plans for you.

Many Christians continue to fellowship with "preventers" and "side-trackers", without recognizing that they are literally spinning their wheels trying to please or help someone else while taking valuable time away from their own destiny.

Boundaries are a huge issue for most Christians, as they feel guilty if they can't keep serving in the church at a certain capacity, or they feel like they are letting God down if they move onto another ministry they feel led to. Guilt and judgement can potentially settle deep within a Christian Body, especially in church congregations without the realization of healthy boundaries. For instance, a church leader may want to help someone with a big need, and that can be a tall order, especially without healthy boundaries. If you are a person that always feels compelled to say "yes" to helping out, without taking a reality check of your family needs and/or the energy needed to come through on commitments, please start looking at recurring patterns, and ask yourself who you are saying "yes" to.

Healthy people in your life will provide balance in your relationship and boost you in your walk with Christ. *Not that you need to only surround yourself with people who will help you create a better life for yourself,* but the last thing you want is to be *trapped* in a personal or professional relationship, where you're being drained of every ounce of energy and purpose you have.

But the truth of our world is that if you're not careful enough or don't know how to recognize toxic people and behaviors, you will find yourself being sucked dry of everything good you have to offer the world as those people use you for their own selfish reasons.

Now, please don't misinterpret what we're saying here. We don't feel the world is all bad and that all people are bad. On the contrary, there is good in everyone, and only through a close and meaningful relationship with God can we all tap into the love within us and the soul of the world to create a better place for us all. However, as you live your life and create one that you love, people with bad or selfish intentions are going to show themselves to you.

It is essential to your survival to know how to recognize people for who they are the moment they tell or show you, communicate effectively, and figure out what and who you like or dislike as soon as possible, so that you can quickly move on or forward. *Identify behaviors and patterns of others; then be ready to describe them and predict outcomes.*

Are you ready to become a master people reader as you build and create an unstoppable life with God as your guide? Then, you're about to learn how to identify some messaging trends and behaviors, giving yourself permission to create boundaries that will improve your life. Enjoy this expert guidance and the pro-tips found inside the following section in this book!

Let's go!

People will always advertise who they are. You just have to be able to see it.

The best way to understand who people are, whether you're just meeting them or have known them for years, is to think of them as advertisements. For example, look at Instagram and branding. You know exactly what a brand is, what they stand for, and what they're up to in the world by just looking at their social media profile.

You can also get that same kind of information about people by looking at their social media. They're advertising who they are if you're paying close enough attention. Whether it's through communication on social media or by the way they text—or don't text—and more, the people in your life are always advertising how important (or unimportant) you are to them both verbally and non-verbally.

If you have someone that always messages you only when they need something from you, whether it's advice, your time, or money, then you know what you're good for to them. If you have another person that checks up on you randomly to see how you're doing or even just to say hi, that's the kind of person you want in your life. They have actually taken the time to care about you without needing anything from you.

In different seasons of your life, you may have a need greater than a friend's need, and that may also reverse in time. Family members who need help may be an exception, as long as you have the energy, and you are not grumbling and complaining about assisting them. When you assist others, you should feel like you are doing what God has called you to do and have a great sense of peace because you are using your gifts to create happiness in other people's lives, "continue to work out your salvation with fear and trembling, for it is God who works in you to will and to act in order to fulfill his good purpose. Do everything without grumbling or arguing." (Philippians 2:12-14)

What are you advertising to others about who you are?

Have you ever taken the time to consider a question like that? It's an important one for your life. What type of energy are you putting out to the world? How are you showing up for the people you say you care about in your life?

Do you have people that you only reach out to when you're in a bind or need something from them? Or are you being a beacon of light in the lives of those you love by checking in on them and taking time to care for them without asking for anything in return?

It is critical to understand how you're showing up for others because if you can't understand how you're showing up for others, how can you see clearly how they're showing up for you? God is the source of everything in your life. Both the specifics of your life and the choices you make are solely on you.

Take some time to look at the message you're putting out to the world. Does it come from a space of love and positivity? Or is it negative and entitled? Do you advertise things such as: "I'm fat," "I'm stupid," "no one likes me," "people leave whenever I come into a room," "I am a drop out," "I quit everything I start," "people better not get on my nerves or I'll go crazy," or "I usually start drama and disappear when people are angry at each other." How can you message and advertise yourself as a confident, loving, caring, responsible, beautiful, authentic, enthusiastic or inspirational human being? Pull from your theme if you need help finding some wonderful ways to describe yourself and skills you have.

Many times, we advertise and message these false things about ourselves because we fear the pain of getting hurt, in making these negative messages about ourselves, we fail to show people where we shine best and miss the opportunity to encourage others. I often joke around about some deficits in my personality or my huge nose, but I really have tried to pull away from this because people will focus on the flaws you tell them rather than the really amazing parts of yourself.

Don't blur yourself. Be clear, consistent, and as comfortable in your own skin as you can. Identifying and combating your own defeating and harmful messages about yourself, that you or someone else created, can prevent you expecting negative outcomes in your life, called a negative self-fulfilling prophecy. Don't you deserve better than a negative version of yourself? Yes, you do! Let's agree to delete these negative messages in your life by identifying them when you say them, writing them down in your journal, and replacing any negative thought with a scripture in the Bible or a positive self affirmation such as: *I am anointed, I am joyful, I am loved, I am focused, I am beautiful, I am valuable, I do not fear evil, God comforts me in all situations, and I am destined for greatness.* [6]

---

[6]   https://gabbyabigaill.com/50-biblical-affirmations-that-will-change-your-life/

What impact does negative messaging have on your life and relationships?

Being constantly in a state of negativity and allowing negative self-talk to run your life can have some pretty devastating consequences. From not being able to see opportunities for what they are to being completely derailed in the face of adversity, challenges, or failures, negative messaging wreaks havoc in your life. Some other consequences of negative messaging in your life include:

Limited thinking: The more you're telling yourself you can't do something, the more you'll believe it. This creates a negative self-fulfilling prophecy which you may be promoting, resulting in the drying up of your opportunities and gifts.

Perfectionism: You start to honestly believe that great isn't as good as perfect and that attaining perfection is the ultimate goal every time you do something. You're constantly in a state of stress trying to achieve perfection, whereas high achievers aren't focused on achieving perfection and, in turn, are less stressed and happier with a job well done. They don't overanalyze and pick apart every aspect of their actions until it's "perfect." And the truth is that most of the time, perfection isn't really perfection anyway, because it's entirely subjective in most cases. I met a young artist that was incredibly talented for her age, she was about 10 years old. She would sketch a beautiful picture and then destroy it. She would start again and get farther in her art work than the previous time and then squish it up and toss it into the trash can. This young and talented girl was so preoccupied with completing perfection that she disabled herself from creating any work of art for weeks. This girl finally surrendered her perfectionism to the Lord and accepted the beauty in her imperfect drawings and that these imperfections were more true to life. Are you judging your masterpiece so much that you can't begin it or complete it? Surrender it to God right now and ask Him to take your anxiety, your negative thoughts on the beauty you are creating, and give Him the paintbrush.

Feelings of depression: There is research that shows that negative self-talk leads to an intensification of feelings of depression. Leaving those feelings unchecked can be pretty damaging in your life. This is where those feelings of not being good enough or that you're not worthy of greatness and the life you want can tear you down until there's nothing left.[7]

Relationship challenges: Living in a state of constant self-criticism creates an energy of constantly appearing that you're needy and insecure. Or even that you tend to turn your negative self-talk into even more negative habits that bother your partner. It creates a lack of communication, and even playfulness can disappear because you're constantly projecting your negative self-criticism into the relationship.

Negative messaging tears apart your life and everything and everyone good in it. You have to find ways to change your messaging to create transformation and breakthroughs in areas you want. And to do that, you have to create positive messaging in your life and relationships.

What are the impacts of positive messaging in your life and relationships?

Positive Messages Make You Happy

Taking the time to start your day with positive messaging—or otherwise known as affirmations—can transform your attitude into a more positive one. Being happy is not as much about how much money and things you have or what you've checked off your bucket list. It's truly about your attitude, outlook on life, and mindset. True happiness comes from within, not from what you have or from external factors. If you depend on others for your happiness, you're always going to be let down. Positive messaging and a positive mindset can awaken your happiness. Ultimately, true happiness comes

---

[7] https://www.nextstep.doctor/overcoming-the-negative-self-talk-cycles-of-depression/

from obedience and faith in the Lord and His instruction book: the Bible.

It Gives You Motivation

Are you looking for a little extra motivation in your daily life to get through the day? Positive messaging at the start of your day helps provide that little extra spark of motivation you need to reach your goals and achieve your dreams. There is nothing quite as powerful as a bit of encouragement to push forward to unlock your full potential. Consider memorizing Bible scripture or posting scripture on your mirror or prayer wall: it can be all that you need to face adversity and overcome the daily obstacles. Starting every day with Jesus means ending your day with the best possible inspired mindset one can obtain.

"I can do all things through Christ who strengthens me" Philippians 4:13

"Greater is He that is in me, than he that is in the world" 1 John 4:4

"No weapon formed again me shall prosper" Isaiah 54:17

"We walk by faith, not by sight" 2 Corinthians 5:7

It Can Increase Your Self Esteem

By consistently choosing to look at yourself in a positive light, you'll more easily discover the confidence and ability to focus on what is good and put more light out into the world. When you have high self-esteem, you naturally think strongly about yourself and, in turn, don't allow negative messaging to get you down. Positive messaging can increase your self-esteem. Start your day by reading a favorite Bible scripture or positive affirmation, and be sure to put out more positive vibes into the universe. Positive vibes create a positive life, higher self-esteem, and acceptance of self-love.

Positive Messages Make You Healthier

Putting out positive messaging into the world helps to elevate your mood and have a healthy impact on your body. Positive thinking actually has the power to give you more energy and reduce your stress levels. Positive messaging comes with many other health benefits, which include:

· Lower rates of depression
· Better psychological and physical well-being
· Better coping skills

The Bible instructs, "Finally, brothers and sisters, whatever is true, whatever is noble, whatever is right, whatever is pure, whatever is lovely, whatever is admirable if anything is excellent or praiseworthy think about such things... And the God of peace will be with you." (Philippians 4:8,9)

Better Relationships With Your Friends And Family
Positive messaging also impacts and affects the people that you surround yourself with. When you're putting out positive energy into your world and tribe, it attracts more positive energy back to you. Focusing on surrounding yourself with good people and positive energy creates opportunities where you can rediscover the joy within you, boost your mood, and create fun everywhere you go. When you live a life filled with positive messaging, you actually have the power to tell people what you want them to think about you without actually having to say anything. How? Because your character, actions, and integrity displayed through your way of life say everything that needs to be said.

Can you see the impacts of negative messaging versus positive messaging in your life? Which type of messaging have you been putting out in your life?

It's essential to really be honest about the answer to that question to be able to take away the most profound experience possible from our time together on this journey.

So, how can you identify what you want and don't want in people?

This is something that has mystified people for ages. How do you know what you want and don't want from the people in your life, your relationships, and even your career?

It's all about the feelings that others, and at times yourself, bring out in you. When you're really in tune with who God says you are, what you want, and what you stand for in your life, your gut and God will guide you. When you experience situations, cycles or thoughts that are contrary to God s absolute best for you, God tells you to move on and toward that which is HIS divine plan and purpose in your life. Listen! "If anyone will not welcome you or listen to your words, leave that home or town and shake the dust off your feet." (Matthew 10:14)

You want to be sure to follow those positive feelings that others bring out in you. If they're negatively charged, they don't fit in your life. If they're positively charged, you want to pursue them and be constantly present to what type of response you have internally to the things, people, and choices in front of you in your life. You want feedback, but you want to make sure you are accepting what the Lord wants you to hear.

A great way to deepen this understanding is by deepening your relationship with God through prayer. Trusting in His guidance along the way and having faith that He's leading you down the path laid out for you can be incredibly freeing. He will bring the people into your life that are needed to achieve the greatness within you and unlock the gifts that you were blessed with when you were created. He will also show you who and what doesn't fit in your life and isn't right for your path. All you have to do is call out in prayer and ask Him when you're unsure. You can do it right where you stand, in that very instant when you're uncertain. Just take a moment, close your eyes and ask him for His guidance. Breathe in God's love and clarity, exhale any anxiety and listen to God's wisdom for you in each situation.

You will be surprised how quickly He will respond and show you the way.

What about communication?

Love comes from communication. Just as you deepen your connection with God and Jesus through prayer and conversation, you deepen your connection to everyone in your life through communication. Developing strong and highly-effective communication strategies can transform your ability to create powerful and impactful relationships in both your personal and professional lives.

Yet so many people struggle with communicating from a space of love. So often, you find yourself making so much effort just wanting to be heard and have your feelings be understood that you don't realize that you're criticizing and cutting down the people you love most.

Here are some expert and highly-effective communication strategies to incorporate into your toolkit for living an unstoppable life from the team at Positive Space.

The Rule of Threes

Have you ever been talking with someone and felt like you couldn't get a word in edgewise? That you're trying to speak or tell a story, and they're constantly interrupting you? The rule of threes is a simple rule to help you be an excellent and effective communicator while also honoring your truth and your time.

If you're interrupted three times, then realize that it was not meant to be said. It could be that it was not meant to be said at that time or that maybe it was not important enough to be told. How can you know which of these it is? Take a step back and evaluate what you were trying to say. It could be that God is actually protecting you from running off the mouth syndrome. You weren't supposed to talk about whatever it was you were sharing yet because He's still working on that part of you or that plan. Whatever the case is, become present with what you were about to share, who you were sharing it with, and why it may not be the time to share it just yet. (Appendix II)

What if I'm the problem?

There's also a rule of three for that too! Have you ever been in a conversation when you start to question yourself in mid-sentence?

Is this person even listening to me? Does this person even care about what I am saying? Why am I saying this? This is where you will use this strategy to evaluate what you are saying. This whole line of questioning is causing you to think about what the other person is thinking while you are trying to verbalize your thoughts. You might have been on track with what you were saying until you started thinking about the other's thoughts, your feelings about what you're sharing, and all of a sudden, you may forget what you were saying, start stuttering, or just quit speaking entirely.

Your three choices when you interrupt yourself are:

- Commit to what you are saying and finish it, do it anyway and own it
- Decide whether or not you will say it. And if you decide not to share but are in mid-sentence, tell those you're sharing with that you don't need to share. Or that it probably was not important.
- If you decide not to share it, you will discover that some people will actually be more inquisitive and want to persuade you to tell them because they now feel like they're missing out on something. It's critical to stay committed and save it for another time, but it is wonderful that the next time you communicate with this person they will be intent on listening to what you are saying.

It's like having three choices in front of you, and it takes that same presence of mind and awareness to know which one is right at that moment in time. Focus on what you're saying. But when you're listening, you want to be sure that you don't focus on what you think or believe the other person is thinking while you're sharing.

Notice when you're sharing something with people who are obviously not interested in what you are saying. And be sure to always share with those that are invested or care about what you are saying, or you're simply wasting your time. Sometimes less is more when you are having a huge struggle communicating with others or processing what you would like to say.

Speaking of less is more...

You were born with two ears and one mouth. There's no greater evidence that God wants you to be present and listen before you speak than that. If He wanted you to speak more than listen, you would've been born with two mouths and one ear.

We're pointing this out because taking the time to be present and listen provides you with some powerful communication tools. It also allows you to more easily identify the advertising that people are doing on or for themselves and what they're about, up to, and after.

By taking the time to listen more and say less, you're able to process what you are hearing from others more effectively. So often, when we communicate with people, we're more focused on how we're going to respond or simply just the act of responding that we don't even actually hear what they've said. We've missed the entire point of the communication or misinterpreted what they're actually communicating. It all goes wrong from there.

Another benefit of this quiet time that comes with saying less and listening more is that you're able to process what you are being called to do by God. It's in the moments of peace, serenity, and quiet that God comes to you. It's where He can communicate with you in a way that you are able and open to hearing His guidance.

In our next chapter, we're going to look at toxic people, how they impact your life, and how to identify them easily.

CHAPTER SIX

TOXIC PEOPLE. RUN!

We have all had toxic people poison our lives. Difficult people are drawn to reasonable people, and all of us have likely had (or have) at least one person in our lives who have us bending around ourselves like barbed wire in endless attempts to please them only to never really get there.

Their damage is found in their ability to be subtle and the way they use the classic response, 'It's not me, it's them.' They leave you questioning yourself. If you're continually hurt or constantly adjusting your own behavior to avoid being hurt, then the chances are it's not you, and it's them.

Being able to spot harmful behavior is the first way to minimize the impact. You may not be able to change what happens, but you can change what you do.

How to identify a toxic person?

They'll keep you guessing about which version of them you're getting.

Toxic people tend to be completely lovely one day, and the next, they'll leave you wondering what in the heck you have done to upset them. There usually isn't any obvious explanation for the change of attitude–you can just tell that something isn't right. They may be sad, cranky, or cold, and then when you ask what's wrong, their answer will likely be something to the effect of 'nothing,' but they'll give you enough sass and passive-aggression to let you know that there is actually something wrong. The 'just enough' may be a heaving sigh, a cold shoulder, or a raised eyebrow. When this happens, you will most likely find yourself making excuses for them and doing everything possible to make them happy. Can you see why they do this?

Don't try to please them. Toxic people have figured out long ago that good people will stop at nothing to keep the people that they love happy. If what you're doing isn't working or isn't making them comfortable for long, it's time to stop. Walk away. You're not responsible for their feelings. If you did something unknowingly to hurt them, ask, talk about it, and if need be, apologize. But you don't have to be left guessing.

They'll manipulate you and the situation.

If you feel like you're truly the only one contributing to your relationship, you're most likely right. Toxic people tend to go out of their way to send out a vibe that you owe them something. They have an innate ability to take from you or hurt you, then instantly say that they were doing it all for you. They seem to twist everything to their benefit while also seeming to present it as an opportunity for you to prove yourself. You don't owe anybody anything. If it doesn't feel like a favor, it's not.

They refuse to own their feelings.

Rather than owning their own feelings, toxic people will act as though the feelings they have are yours. They project their feelings onto you and play them off as if you're the one feeling them. For instance, someone who is upset but won't take any responsibility for their upset may end up accusing you of being angry with them.

When this happens, you'll always be left in the position of justifying and defending yourself. This goes on and on and often in circles. Because it's not actually about you, it's about them. Therefore, it's critical to be crystal clear about what's yours and theirs. If you're constantly defending yourself, you are being projected on. Remember that you don't have to explain, justify or defend yourself, or deal with continually being accused of feelings that aren't actually yours.

They'll make you prove yourself to them.

Toxic people constantly put you in positions where you have to choose between them and something else. And you will always feel that you have to choose them. They have an incredible talent of being able to wait until you have a commitment, then they'll unpack the drama on you and make you choose them over the other thing that you care about too. The problem here is that enough will never be enough.

They never apologize.

They'll lie before they ever apologize to you. And what that means is there's really no point in arguing with them. Instead, they'll twist the story and change the way it happened. They may even retell it so convincingly that they'll have you believing their nonsense.

People don't have to apologize when they're wrong. And the best part is that you don't need an apology to move forward with your life. Simply move forward without them. Don't ever surrender your truth to keep the argument going. There's no point.

They'll be there in a crisis but never share your joy.

Toxic people find reasons for your good news to not be great news. The classics: About a promotion–'The money isn't that great for the amount of work you'll be doing.' About a holiday at the beach–'Well, it will be very hot. Are you sure you want to go?' About being made Queen of the Universe–'Well, the Universe isn't that big, you know, and I'm pretty sure you won't get tea breaks.' Get the idea? Don't let them dampen you or shrink you down to their size. You don't need their approval anyway–or anyone else's, for that matter.

They'll leave a conversation unfinished–and then they'll go offline.

They don't pick up their phone. They don't answer texts. And in between rounds of their voicemail message, you may find that you're playing the argument repeatedly in your head. This just leaves you guessing about the status of your relationship, wondering what you've done, or even if they're dead, alive, or simply ignoring you. This is all control. They're controlling your mind and your life without actually being in it at that time. People that love and care about you won't leave you in the abyss like that.

They'll use non-toxic words with a toxic tone.

The message may be innocent enough, but it will be conveyed much more by their tone. Something like, 'What did you do today?' can mean vastly diffcrent things depending on how they say it. It can mean anything from 'I'm sure you did nothing as usual' to 'I'm positive that your day was better than mine. Mine was bad. Really bad. And you didn't even ask me about it.' When you question their tone, they fight right back with something like, 'I only asked what did you do today,' which is kind of true, but is it really?

They'll bring irrelevant detail into a conversation.

When you are trying to resolve something vital to you, toxic people sprinkle in irrelevant details from ten arguments ago. Before you know it, you find yourself arguing about something you did a year ago, still defending yourself, and never actually dealing with the issue at hand. Somehow, it just always seems to end up about what you've done to them.

They'll make it about how you're talking rather than what you're talking about.

You might be trying to resolve an issue or get clarification. Before you know it, the conversation or argument has moved away from the vital issue to how you talked about it—whether there is an issue with your manner or not. You'll find yourself defending your tone, gestures, choice of words, or the way your belly moves when you breathe—it doesn't even need to make sense. Meanwhile, your initial need has gone on the pile of unfinished conversations that grow bigger by the day.

They exaggerate.

'You always ...' 'You never ....' It's hard to defend yourself against this form of manipulation. Toxic people have a way of drawing on the one time you didn't or the one time you did as evidence of your shortcomings. So don't buy into the argument. You won't win. And you don't need to.

They are judgmental.

Sometimes, we all get it wrong, but toxic people will make sure you know it. Then, they'll judge you and swipe at your self-esteem, suggesting that you're less than them because you made a mistake. Of course, we're all allowed to get it wrong now and then, but unless we've done something that affects them, nobody has the right to stand in judgment.

Remove toxic people from your life as quickly as you can. They only tear you down and suck the life out of you. You can find out more about how to identify and remove toxic people from your life on my YouTube channel here.

CHAPTER SEVEN

HEARING THE MASTER'S VOICE

In this digital age, we're surrounded by voices, and they're not always good. So it's essential to be able to decipher God's voice from among the constant barrage of noise and voices from the outside world.

Whether you're spending time constantly scrolling through your phone on social media, talking with your loved ones, or watching the news, if you can't hear your own voice, how do you know what life you want to live?

Chances are, you don't. You have to be able to bring peace and silence to your life and listen to God's voice in your life. So put down the phone, turn off the TV, check out from the digital distractions, and spend time in the Word.

Learning how to be still can transform your relationship with God.

If you're stuck in your life and unsure what to do next, one of the best things you can do is to be still. When you're still, and life is at a standstill around you, it's best to trust in His plan and spend time in the Word and with His spirit.

What the Bible says about being still?

Being still in today's world is far more easily said than done. There's always just so much happening around you. But have you ever stopped to wonder how you can go through so much pain and suffering and still find joy? It only comes from being still. When you're still, it means that you've put all of your worries in God's hands. "Cast all your anxiety on him because he cares for you." (1 Peter 5:7)

Instead of constantly letting your worries take over and control your world, you're listening to the voice of the Lord and His guidance. You're not to let your joy come from outside influences and things because they are temporary. True unadulterated joy comes from Him, "The joy of the Lord is your strength." (Nehemiah 8:10)

The Lord always remains the same. He is a constant. He is loyal. He is omnipotent. He is loving. When you allow your joy to come from Jesus, you can finally find stillness and stop letting the storm take over your world.

He has proved time and time again that He can calm any storm you're faced with. There are times when God will allow trials to come into your life so you can cut your armor and your character and learn to be more trusting of Him and His plan. God says, "I'm in control. I can do all things. Stop fearing and trust in me instead."

If you're constantly allowing your thoughts to run rampant, don't go further down the rabbit hole of seeking guidance and help from temporary fixes and sources. Go to God. Bring Him your worries and concerns, and He will take them and carry the burden of them for you so you can be still.

When you stop and focus on the love and beauty of the Lord, you're able to finally receive the peace beyond all understanding that He has promised you.

So, what does the Bible say about being still?

Verses regarding the practice of being still and quiet before God.

1. Zechariah 2:13 Be still before the LORD, all mankind, because he has roused himself from his holy dwelling.

2. Psalm 46:10-11 Be still and know that I am God! I will be honored by every nation. I will be honored throughout the world. The LORD of Heaven's Armies is here among us; the God of Israel is our fortress.

3. Exodus 14:14 The LORD will fight for you while you keep still.

4. Habakkuk 2:20 The LORD is in his holy Temple. All the earth— be quiet in his presence.

Verses about how Jesus can calm the storm within you and around you.

5. Mark 4:39-41 He got up, rebuked the wind, and said to the waves, "Quiet! Be still!" Then the wind died down, and it was completely calm. He said to his disciples, "Why are you so afraid? Do you still have no faith?" They were terrified and asked each other, "Who is this? Even the wind and the waves obey him!"

6. Psalm 107:28-29 Then they cried out to the LORD in their trouble, and he brought them out of their distress. He stilled the storm to a whisper; the waves of the sea were hushed.

7. Psalm 46:1-7 God is our refuge and strength, a great help in times of distress. Therefore, we will not be frightened when the earth roars, when the mountains shake in the depths of the seas, when its waters roar and rage, when the mountains tremble despite their pride. Look! There is a river whose streams make the city of God rejoice, even the Holy Place of the Most High. Since God is in her midst, she will not be shaken. God will help her at the break of dawn. The nations roared; the kingdoms were shaken. His voice boomed; the earth melts. The Lord of the heavenly armies is with us; our refuge is the God of Jacob.

Verses about stopping everything and putting your focus on the Lord.

8. 1 Samuel 12:16 Now then, stand still and see this great thing the LORD is about to do before your eyes!

9. Exodus 14:13 But Moses told the people, "Don't be afraid. Just stand still and watch the LORD rescue you today. The Egyptians you see today will never be seen again."

Verses about waiting patiently and putting your complete trust in the Lord.

11. Psalm 37:7 Be still in the presence of the LORD, and wait patiently for him to act. Don't worry about evil people who prosper or fret about their wicked schemes.

12. Psalm 62:5-6 Let all that I am wait quietly before God, for my hope is in him. He alone is my rock and my salvation, my fortress where I will not be shaken.

13. Isaiah 40:31 But they that wait upon the LORD shall renew their strength; they shall mount up with wings as eagles; they shall run, and not be weary, and they shall walk, and not faint.

14. James 5:7-8 Therefore, brothers, be patient until the Lord's coming. See how the farmer waits for the precious fruit of the earth and is patient with it until it receives the early and the late rains. You also must be patient. Strengthen your hearts because the Lord's coming is near.

What about when you're faced with hard times?

God has you covered there too!

17. John 16:33 I have told you this so that through me you may have peace. In the world, you'll have trouble, but be courageous—I've overcome the world!

18. Psalm 23:4 Even when I must walk through the darkest valley, I fear no danger, for you are with me; your rod and your staff reassure me.

19. Romans 12:12 Rejoice in hope, be patient in tribulation, be constant in prayer.

If you give it to God, it will come back to you.

This is one of the most significant truths about your relationship with God. What you give comes back to you. So when something bad happens to you, give something and change the trajectory of your day by paying it forward.

The energy that you put out into the world comes back to you. So you're literally creating your future by being the person you already want to be now. And by putting that energy into the world, you're creating the space for it to come rushing back to you.

For instance, if you're blessed with money, you can use it to brighten someone's day, and it immediately distracts you from anger and bitterness.

Now that we've covered all of that, we wanted to close out *Christian Focus In A Blurry World* by sharing some truths found within the Word and how you can use them in your own life today. Because you cannot create a life well lived and loved without having God at the center of it all.

CHAPTER EIGHT

LIVING WITH GOD AT YOUR CENTER.

Part of living a God-centered life means understanding all of the tools and lessons for living that can be found within His Word. So let's spend some time in the Word and discover firsthand all of the blessings that lie before you when you accept Jesus as your Lord and Savior and lead a life with Him.

The full armor of God protects you everywhere you go.

Living with the full armor of God provides you with a level of protection for your mind, body, and spirit that can't be found anywhere else in the world. Here is a collection of verses that reference and share the greatness that is found when you put on the full armor of God in your life.

Ephesians 6:10-18

10. Finally, be strong in the Lord and in his mighty power. 11. Put on the full armor of God so that you can take your stand against the devil's schemes. 12. For our struggle is not against flesh and blood, but against the rulers, against the authorities, against the powers of this dark world, and against the spiritual forces of evil in the heavenly realms. 13. Therefore, put on the full armor of God, so that when the day of evil comes, you may be able to stand your ground, and after you have done everything, to stand. 14. Stand firm then, with the belt of truth buckled around your waist, with the breastplate of righteousness in place. 15. And with your feet fitted with the readiness that comes from the gospel of peace. 16. In addition to all this, take up the shield of faith, with which you can extinguish all the flaming arrows of the evil one. 17. Take the helmet of salvation and the sword of the Spirit, which is the Word of God.

18 And pray in the Spirit on all occasions with all kinds of prayers and requests. With this in mind, be alert and always keep on praying for all the Lord's people.

Hebrews 4:12

For the Word of God is living and active, sharper than any two-edged sword, piercing to the division of soul and of spirit, of joints and of marrow, and discerning the thoughts and intentions of the heart.

Isaiah 59:17

He put on righteousness as a breastplate, and a helmet of salvation on his head; he put on garments of vengeance for clothing and wrapped himself in zeal as a cloak.

How about bravery or courage?

Throughout the Word, God commands us to fear not, to have courage in our lives, and to be of good cheer. But there are times when you may doubt your own strength and conviction, and those are the times when it's essential to turn to the scripture.

Here is a collection of Bible verses about bravery and courage in the face of any challenge that comes your way.

1 Chronicles 28:20

David also said to Solomon, his son, "Be strong and courageous and do the work. Do not be afraid or discouraged, for the LORD God, my God, is with you. He will not fail you or forsake you until all the work for the service of the temple of the LORD is finished.

1 Corinthians 15:58

Therefore, my dear brothers and sisters, stand firm. Let nothing move you. Always give yourselves fully to the work of the Lord because you know that your labor in the Lord is not in vain.

Isaiah 54:4

Do not be afraid; you will not be put to shame. Do not fear disgrace; you will not be humiliated. You will forget the shame of your youth and remember no more the reproach of your widowhood.

Isaiah 41:10-13

So do not fear, for I am with you; do not be dismayed, for I am your God. I will strengthen you and help you; I will uphold you with my righteous right hand. All who rage against you will surely be ashamed and disgraced; those who oppose you will be as nothing and perish. Though you search for your enemies, you will not find them. Those who wage war against you will be as nothing at all. For I am the LORD your God who takes hold of your right hand and says to you, "Do not fear; I will help you."

What does the Bible say about fellowship at church?

You can find many instances within the Word about fellowship with your brothers and sisters at church, but there is one verse that we love to reference here at Positive Space.

Hebrews 10:24-25

And let us consider how we may spur one another on toward love and good deeds, not giving up meeting together, as some are in the habit of doing, but encouraging one another—and all the more as you see the Day approaching. If you are looking for a perfect church, stop looking, and if you find one, don't join it, because you will ruin it.

Forgiveness is everything.

Forgiveness is the most critical aspect and characteristic of living a Godly life. You must learn to release yourself from anger. Holding onto anger and refusing to forgive is toxic to you. It literally poisons you.

One of the best things you can do for yourself is to surrender the person you're refusing to forgive to the Lord and realize that you have hurt people as well, and you don't want the Lord to judge you for your mistakes.

Here is a collection of some of the most profound and compelling Bible verses about forgiveness and its power in your life.

2 Chronicles 7:14

If my people who are called by my name humble themselves, and pray and seek my face and turn from their wicked ways, then 1 will hear from heaven and will forgive their sin and heal their land.

Isaiah 55:7

Let the wicked forsake his way, and the unrighteous man his thoughts; let him return to the Lord, that he may have compassion for him, and to our God, for he will abundantly pardon.

Psalm 103:12

As far as the east is from the west, so far has he removed our transgressions from us.

Matthew 18: 21-22

Then Peter came to Jesus and asked, "Lord, how many times shall I forgive my brother or sister who sins against me? Up to seven times?" Jesus answered, "I tell you, not seven times, but seventy-seven times."

Matthew 6: 14-15

For if you forgive other people when they sin against you, your heavenly Father will also forgive you. But if you do not forgive others their sins, your Father will not forgive your sins.

Work hard and play hard because you never know when life will go away!

Life is temporary and fleeting. It's here, and then it's gone as quickly as it came. Are you ready to meet your Maker whenever that time comes?

Are you going to live your best life until your last dying day? Then, what are you going to do with your remaining time? Isn't it time that you created a life you love and live it fully each and every day that you have left in this world?

You deserve to have a life you love and to live it to the fullest. After all, the Bible tells us many times that the world as we know it will end, and the end times will bring a reckoning. Whether you're going to see those end times while you're on this planet or not, the one truth of all of this is that you are guaranteed death, and you cannot escape it no matter what you do.

Here's a little something the Lord says about the end times and that reckoning.

Matthew 24:36-44

36. "But about that day or hour no one knows, not even the angels in heaven, nor the Son, but only the Father. 37. As it was in the days of Noah, so it will be at the coming of the Son of Man. 38. For in the

days before the flood, people were eating and drinking, marrying and giving in marriage, up to the day Noah entered the ark; 39. And they knew nothing about what would happen until the flood came and took them all away. That is how it will be at the coming of the Son of Man. 40. Two men will be in the field; one will be taken and the other left. 41. Two women will be grinding with a hand mill; one will be taken and the other left. 42. Therefore keep watch, because you do not know on what day your Lord will come. 43. But understand this: If the owner of the house had known at what time of night the thief was coming, he would have kept watch and would not have let his house be broken into. 44. So you also must be ready because the Son of Man will come at an hour when you do not expect him."

Are you ready to meet your Maker?

It's time to breathe in God's love.

When you receive Jesus as your Lord and Savior, you commit your life to Jesus Christ and to live with the Lord at the center of everything you do.

You also equip yourself with the awesome power of prayer and the guidance of God as you create a life you love. So whether you were washed over by the Holy Spirit at a younger age and are returning just as the Prodigal Son did, or you want to breathe in God's love for the first time, there is a quick prayer you can pray right now to commit your life to Jesus Christ.

Doing so will equip you with all of the tools, training, and guidance that we've discussed in the pages of this book so you can finally heal from the past, align with the present and achieve profound clarity to cultivate a wonderful, empowering future.

The Sinner's Prayer
At Positive Space, we celebrate getting closer to Jesus Christ and be in true fellowship with Him. If you did not take the opportunity

to receive Jesus into your heart or renew your heart earlier in this book, would you like to do so now? Take time to say this prayer to Him and know that you are at peace because you are in His will.

"Jesus, I believe you are the Son of God, that you died on the cross to rescue me from sin and death and to restore me to the Father. I choose now to turn from my sins, my self-centeredness, and every part of my life that does not please you. I choose you. I give myself to you. I receive your forgiveness and ask you to take your rightful place in my life as my Savior and Lord. Come reign in my heart, fill me with your love and your life, and help me to become a person who is truly loving—a person like you. Restore me, Jesus. Live in me. Love through me. Thank you, God. In Jesus' name, I pray. Amen."

We hope that this book has been a beautiful journey through the Holy Spirit and has helped you find meaning, passion, and purpose in your life. For more information about how the team at Positive Space can help you transform your life, be sure to check out our website <u>here</u>.

the 25% Rule

25%
Of the people you
meet will like you
right away &
continue to like you.

25%
Of the people you
meet will like you,
but will not like
you over time.

25%
Of the people you
meet will not like
you, but will like
you over time.

25%
Of the people you
meet will not like you.

David Guerra

Rules Of 3

When You Are Interrupted

In each of these rules, God is giving you a way out to stop sharing and/or extra time to process what you decide to share with others

Stop what you are trying to communicate because:	Stop what you are trying to communicate & evaluate how you will proceed:
Interrupted by others 3 times	Interrupted by your thinking
It was not meant to be said	Commit to what you are saying and finish it
It was not meant to be said at this time and place	Stop speaking and let your listeners know you will tell them on another occasion, now is not the time or place
It was not important	Stop speaking and let your listeners know that you decided the story or what you were saying was not important

Rami Donahoe

ACKNOWLEDGEMENTS

MAHALO NUI LOA

To my brilliant husband Chris: Thank you for all your love, support, humor and most of all for being a man of God! **Isaiah 41:10**

Mahalo to my mother, Gloria Davis, for her strength in Christ and introducing me to Jesus. Your inspirational music and Biblical knowledge have given me wisdom through my whole life. **Revelation 21:4, 1 Corinthians 10:13**

This book is dedicated to my dear adventurers Rylie and Cambell: may you use this guide to get through tough times and tough people. **Joshua 1:9**

Thank you to my beautiful sisters and brothers at The Church At Koloa, especially Pastor Harold Kilborn, Pastor Christine Kilborn and Pastor Jodie Johns for showing the love of Jesus Christ daily to every human you encounter. Mahalo to Youth Pastors Isaiah and Melissa Jones for your energetic, loving and Biblical program! **Matthew 6:33**

Special thanks to Pastor Monica Zenger, Pastor Scott Zenger, Pastor Steve Franks, Pastor Victoria Franks, Pastor Vince and Pastor Ava Venson, Kuulei Palau & Ohana, Bobie-Li Orsatelli & Ohana, Shintani Ohana, Ministers Bryson and Crystal Garma (Kings Chapel Kauai & Alaska). **Isaiah 40:31**

"You refresh my spirit and you deserve recognition" **1 Corinthians 16:18**

Blessings to Colleen Tehero & Ohana, Matsusaka Ohana & Moriwake Ohana **Hebrews 1:14**

Love and blessings to the Samonte Ohana **1 Corinthians 10:13**

Mahalo to my Sister In Christ Robbi Castillo-Contrades. You are loving and generous to all of your students and show the love of Christ in your ministry at school and through your music. Thank you to the whole Contrades familia: Kaipo, Victoria, Alyssa and Courtney. **Philippians 4:6, 7**

Blessings and mahalo to: Analiza, Jake Corpuz, Thyra and Troy Corpuz for your loving smiles and encouragement. Danke schön to Georg Renges, Sebastian Renges, Jon Reed and the Huntington Beach Freedom Bungalow. A big mahalo to the Tapia Ohana Of Kauai. Mahalo to Diana Antis **1 John 4:4**

Thank you to my Fountain Valley First Christian Church Ohana Mike & Stacie Strout, you are so loved and appreciated **Romans 15:13**

Mahalo to Nerio, Alida, Kainalu & Kaimana Lazaro, Betsy and Edwin Shinagawa, Percy Taboniar, Keoni, DeeAnn and Kealohi Pau, Michelle Kaauamo, Indulekha Elizabeth Reeves, Mason Ganiron, Unique Divine, Heather, Eternity and Gabe Catchpole, Dana, Rory & Ikaika Salazar. The blessed and highly favored: Gaylord Kaohi & Joy Abreu-Kaohi & Mark and Diane Beeksma **Jeremiah 29:11**

Mahalo to my inspirational friends: Dr. Sherene McHenry, Dr. Valerie Willman, Toni Shibiyama & Gregory Shepherd **Psalm 37:4**

Mahalo for your musical inspiration Lois Ricciardi & Virginia Shepherd **1 Chronicles 15:16**

To Teighlor and Joseph Abreu: The Lord will never leave you. You are strong warriors in Christ Jesus! **Romans 8:37**

Made in the USA
Columbia, SC
28 July 2022

64075013R00057